George ~~Benton~~

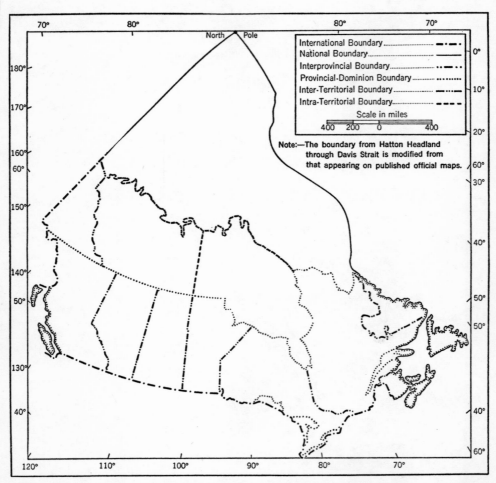

Figure 1. The major political boundaries of Canada. The eastern part of the Arctic sector boundary from Cape Chidley to 60 degrees east is only approximate.

CANADA
DEPARTMENT OF MINES AND TECHNICAL SURVEYS

GEOGRAPHICAL BRANCH

MEMOIR 2

THE BOUNDARIES OF CANADA, ITS PROVINCES AND TERRITORIES

BY

Norman L. Nicholson

EDMOND CLOUTIER, C.M.G., O.A., D.S.P.
QUEEN'S PRINTER AND CONTROLLER OF STATIONERY
OTTAWA, 1954.

Price, 75 cents

88589—1½

CONTENTS

CHAPTER VII

CHAPTER VIII

CHAPTER IX

CHAPTER X

CHAPTER XI

APPENDIX

Illustrations

PREFACE

When the United States Geological Survey, which was at that time responsible for much of the geographical analysis of the country, published its pioneer work on boundaries in 1885, it did much to focus attention on the geographical problems associated with boundary location. Since then, professional geographers, such as Dr. Boggs in the State Department, Dr. Jones of Yale University, and others, have advanced the geographical study of boundaries very considerably.

The need for corresponding work in Canada, particularly on the provincial boundaries, has long been felt. With the union of Newfoundland and Canada, it seemed appropriate to make an appraisal of the situation. This memoir is the result.

It is essentially a geographical appraisal. Historical, political, and economic factors are necessarily analysed and considered, but the emphasis has been upon the geographical reasons for, descriptions of, and results of, boundary location.

Boundaries have always been of peculiar interest to geographers, for geography is the study of the spatial distributions that go to make the surface of the earth what it is. Early geographers measured the bounds of land and sea. Later they plotted in the boundaries of the great climatic zones. Much later they concerned themselves with the boundaries between races and religions. In modern times they are interested in every kind of boundary, physical, economic, social, or political, that may have an effect upon the geography of the land, or may derive from it.

Unfortunately, perhaps, the popular idea is that physical boundaries are much more real than human ones and are, therefore, more geographical or, at any rate, more rewarding of study by the geographers. Much has been made of the influence of the great physiographic boundaries upon the development of Canada. It is true that these—the Appalachian front, the edge of the Canadian Shield, the "steps" of the Prairies, and the Cordilleran front—have played a very great role in Canadian affairs. The Appalachians have more or less divided off the Maritimes from the central provinces; the Shield has tended to divide the densely settled parts of the central provinces from the Prairies; and the Cordilleras have separated the Prairies from the Pacific coast.

It is also true that climatic boundaries have had a great effect on Canadian population. The climatic limit of the growth of wheat did much to determine the settlement of the Prairies. Climate is still one of the principal factors affecting the line of the northern frontier.

Yet although the influence of physiographic, climatic, edaphic, and biotic boundaries is considerable, it is by no means the whole of geography. It may not even be the greater part of geography. Human boundaries are often more important than physical ones in changing the landscape. Indeed, very frequently they transcend and supersede the physical ones. Thus, on the Quebec side of the Ottawa River, the French-Canadian system of land division and the uninuclear settlements typical of that province have created a landscape that is highly characteristic and is notably different from that on the Ontario side, with its different system of land division and multi-nuclear settlements. Thus a valley that forms a major natural region is actually divided into two cultural landscapes and is in effect made up of two geographical entities. In the normal course of events the river would draw the two sides of the valley together and become the very axis of unification. In the human geography of the area it is the frontier of separation.

There are other examples of this in Canada, and many more in other parts of the world. They are enough to show that quite immaterial things like cultural, legal, and political systems can have a profound material effect upon the development and condition of the land.

In studying boundaries, four basic questions arise, namely: where does the boundary occur; when and under what circumstances did it take shape; what influenced its location; how does it affect the land? A fifth question would be, has it changed, and if so where, when, and how?

It is relatively easy to indicate where existing boundaries are, but in a survey of past boundaries difficulties are experienced, either because the boundaries were not too clearly defined, and sometimes not mapped, or because the maps were not accurate. An attempt has been made in this memoir to show the boundaries as they actually existed. As the international boundaries have been adequately treated, in the main, attention is focused chiefly on the provincial and territorial ones.

In a growing country like Canada, boundaries have frequently changed in accordance with new situations and needs. Therefore, their development is an indication of the development of the country. Indeed, they are, in a way, the summation of the development that has gone on and that has called for final definition and recognition on the ground. The memoir traces the main changes in this light.

What affected the actual location of the boundary appeared usually to be a compromise between various political and economic forces. Naturally, these forces did not work in a vacuum, but had to take cognizance of the terrain. Geography played a significant role in locating the boundary.

However, we must here distinguish between what the people at the time thought to be the geography of the country and its actual geography. In earlier times, boundaries were often drawn on the basis of the imagined geography of the area, because not too much was known and maps were very sketchy and inadequate. In fact, it was partly to get around this difficulty that treaty makers and the makers of provincial boundaries often used parallels of latitude or meridians of longitude. This was convenient, but meant, of course, that later on the boundary concerned usually bore little relationship to the economy of the area.

The attempt to draw "natural" rather than "artificial" boundaries was made in places, but again ideas of what a natural boundary was changed. Rivers were thought to be natural boundaries, and, where they were reinforced by ethnic and cultural divisions, were so; otherwise they were seen to become axes of intercourse, not frontiers of division.

Signs were not lacking that the economy of a region was taken into account and, particularly in Labrador, northwest Ontario, northern Manitoba, and southern Saskatchewan and Alberta, the economic geography of the times had its influence. One of the most interesting questions to arise in these cases was whether a boundary should be drawn to enclose a single-economy area or a multiple-economy one. In northwest Ontario and southern Saskatchewan and Alberta the arguments for making provinces coincide with the lumberman's or with the rancher's domain were pressed quite far. However, events would seem to have favoured the inclusion of several different belts of country, with different climates, and with the possibility of developing different economies, in one political unit. Although such a unit might have many more political problems to deal with than those of one occupation group, it would benefit by greater economic differentiation and stability. The life of the province would, in other words, be enriched by its differences.

That this custom prevailed may have done much towards enriching the life of the country as a whole. Undoubtedly, the kind of boundary drawn has far-reaching effects on the kind of development, social as well as economic, that may evolve. In fact, in the long run, boundaries probably make, rather than are made by, geography. No doubt the geographical factors that are partly responsible for their birth continue to be real. This is especially true of the international boundaries, which are later exaggerated in importance as immigration and tariff boundaries. Nevertheless, once the boundary is drawn, the political use of the space bounded by it leads to an orientation of route-ways, a choice of sites for settlements, policies of resource development, programs of colonization, and so forth, that profoundly affect the human geography of the area.

This memoir has indicated some of these changes and suggested others, but, on the whole, has left the question of the geographical effects of boundaries for further study. The main purpose has been to describe the evolution and location of the boundaries, to analyse the associated problems, and to classify the types of boundaries that have arisen in Canada. It is clear that many aspects of these boundaries still remain unsolved, but it is hoped that future workers may see the trends and problems more readily and may direct their efforts towards their fuller elucidation.

J. WREFORD WATSON,
Director, Geographical Branch

The Boundaries of Canada, Its Provinces and Territories

CHAPTER I

INTRODUCTION

GENERAL STATEMENT

The study of boundaries is one aspect of the field of political geography, which is concerned with the relationships between the earth and political areas. If a political area is regarded as any piece of the earth's surface possessing governmental unity, then boundaries may be regarded as one of the basic elements of such an area. Boundaries in this sense are man-made. They are much more than lines on a map; they are functional, cultural features planted on a physical landscape, vitally related to their bordering regions (84, p. 54)[1].

As the modern state evolved, and the demand for the establishment of clear-cut boundaries arose, it became more and more necessary to know where the territory of one state ended and that of another began. Parallel with this development, however, came the problem of the increasing complexity of administration within the state. Members of a central government could not be expected to be sufficiently familiar with all the requirements of different parts of the state, hence the growth of the practice of delegating power to local authorities, whose areas of administration also called for boundaries. The necessity of boundary lines has, therefore, come with the growth of organized society, the pressure of population on resources, and the lifting and widening of the material standards of living (14, p. 217), and thus the frontier became reduced, legally, to a line.

A further development was the growth of federal states, essentially combinations of states already organized and having their own external and internal boundaries. Although federation inevitably diminished the autonomy of the participating states, it did not eliminate them, and their boundaries usually remained unchanged. A federal system implies, by its very definition, an aggregation of local governing units, each exercising certain separate powers but conceding others to the central or federal government (33, p. 91). Canada is such a federated state and hence its political map presents a web of boundary lines, each of which marks the limit of territory within which an administrative unit exercises authority. The fact that several federal states (e.g., the United States of America) are states composed of former sovereign states makes it necessary to distinguish the completely sovereign state by capitalizing the word. When reference is made to a component part this is not done.

"By sovereignty is meant the authority of the State to have control of, or rule over, the territory and persons and objects present there. Within the territory the State exercises its legislative power, its administration of justice and its administrative authority" (162, p. 10). Canada, being a federal state, has divided some aspects of sovereignty between the Federal Government and the Provincial Governments. The provincial boundaries determine for millions of people the ideas their children shall be taught in school and the language in which they shall be taught. In Canada, education is a provincial matter, and every province has a different school system and a different syllabus of subjects.

---

[1] Numbers, etc., in parentheses refer to Chapter XI, page 124.

Boundaries can also determine the books, newspapers, and magazines that people shall be able to buy and read; the kind of money they shall use; the markets in which they must buy and sell; and the kinds of food they eat (10, p. 5). For example, the sale of margarine is prohibited in the province of Quebec but permitted in the province of Ontario. To at least some extent, boundaries may restrict the movements of people, the exchange of goods, of money, even of ideas. There is no sharp line of division between the functions of international and internal boundaries (10, p. 4), but the magnitude of the effect of boundaries on persons and things must vary with the degree of authority of the political unit and the extent of the administrative powers exercised within it. As such authority decreases, so the effects of boundaries decrease, and thus, even from this point of view, there must be different types of boundaries, depending on the degree of their effects or functions.

In Canada, each administrative authority has its territorial limits defined by boundaries. A piece of land owned by an individual has its boundaries, within which that individual may exercise certain authority. His land, however, is subject to the local governing body, and this in turn is responsible to a provincial authority, which is itself, in the last analysis, responsible to the authority of the State.

Thus the State "Canada" is first delimited by boundaries. Some of these are boundaries with other States or major political units. These are usually "nations" but may be territories controlled by a nation, such as Alaska. These boundaries are usually referred to as international boundaries. International boundaries may be coextensive with the boundaries of federally controlled land, such as the Yukon Territory. The 141st Meridian separates not only Canada and Alaska but also Yukon Territory and Alaska. Usually, however, the International Boundary is coextensive with provincial boundaries. The 49th Parallel separates Canada and the United States as well as British Columbia, Alberta, Saskatchewan, and most of Manitoba from the United States. The remaining boundaries of Canada are the seaward boundaries of the territorial waters and are usually referred to as "national boundaries".

Canada is, however, made up of ten provinces and two territories, each of which has its own boundaries. Not all of these boundaries separate areas with similar administrative functions. Some are true interprovincial boundaries, such as the boundary between Alberta and Saskatchewan. Sometimes, however, a boundary separates a province from a territory or from Canadian territorial waters. As the last two are under the direct jurisdiction of the Federal Government, such boundaries might be termed "federal-provincial". Although, as has been pointed out, provincial boundaries may coincide with international boundaries, a provincial boundary can never be coextensive with a purely national boundary because all navigable waters are under the control of the Federal Government. Another type of boundary separates two adjacent territories, such as the boundary between Yukon and the Northwest Territories. As both areas are under federal control, the boundary between them might be described as inter-territorial. Finally, there are boundaries within the territories, such as that between Mackenzie and Keewatin, that can be called "intra-territorial" boundaries. Figure 1 illustrates a classification along these lines.

Then each province is further subdivided into municipalities, which vary from province to province. In Prince Edward Island, Nova Scotia, New Brunswick, Ontario, and Quebec the first order of municipalities is made up of counties, which are further subdivided into cities, towns, villages, and townships, although there are minor variations even here. In Newfoundland and the four western provinces the two orders of municipalities are lacking. Instead, the municipalities are either rural or urban, the latter being made up of cities, towns, and villages, but again with minor variations.

But no matter how the municipalities are arranged, the smallest of them includes a multitude of further boundaries that mark the limits of private property held either by individuals or corporations. Even these may have boundaries within them that represent the limits of the smallest economic units, such as fields or city lots.

PREVIOUS WORK

Studies of international boundaries are much more common than those of the internal boundaries of states. This is particularly true of Canada, and the reports of the International Boundary Commission are authoritative, comprehensive, well-documented, and well illustrated.

The only comprehensive approach to the major internal boundaries of a federal State seems to have been made by the United States Geological Survey. A bulletin on this subject was published as long ago as 1885. This has been enlarged and revised five times since then, the latest edition appearing in 1932 (49).

But although literature on Canadian boundaries, both international and internal, is by no means lacking, it has never been collected and correlated. White (193) came close to doing so, but dealt most intensively with the international boundaries of Canada. There have been several notable studies of the boundaries of individual provinces and regions. Ganong's monograph on the boundaries of New Brunswick, which was published in 1901 (52), will long remain a classic in its field. Ireland (82) dealt with the boundaries of British Columbia, and Bériault (6) with problems that directly relate to political boundaries in the Canadian Arctic. But demarcation and the geographical setting of boundaries have generally been ignored, Jones (85, 87) and Dagenais (30) being among the few to have published geographical studies of any parts of Canada's present boundaries.

THE PRESENT STUDY AND ACKNOWLEDGMENTS

In this memoir, as Canada's international boundaries have an extensive literature, and as municipal and local boundaries are of strictly local importance, emphasis has been directed chiefly towards the various provincial and territorial boundaries. But even here it was neither possible nor desirable to deal fully with every detail of certain boundary controversies; a selection only has been made in order to show how boundary problems have been dealt with in Canada in varying circumstances. Thus, the Ontario-Manitoba boundary is taken as an example of an interprovincial problem; the Canada-Newfoundland boundary controversy as an example of an international problem, and also, uniquely, one concerning primarily two members of the Commonwealth. The solution of the New Brunswick-Quebec boundary dispute rested partly on an international agreement as well as an interprovincial one, and the boundaries between Alberta, Saskatchewan, and Manitoba exemplify modern boundary establishment in very recently developed areas. Thus, with this somewhat restricted objective, no attempt has been made to present a full statement of events that were concerned with boundaries in what is now Canada, but only those that appear to be significant in understanding the pattern of evolution of these boundaries and in determining the relationship between this evolution and modern geographical principles.

It is also on this basis that the selection and method of presentation of the maps is made. The maps on discovery and exploration, for example, are not intended to portray every detail or to show every voyage and journey made. The intention is rather to show the *extent* of the first most important expeditions and the parts of present-day Canada that were covered or touched upon.

During the course of this work every interprovincial boundary, with the exception of the Quebec-Newfoundland, has been crossed at least once and the geographical situation on either side examined. In addition, the International Boundary has been crossed and surveyed in a similar way at several points, and the Keewatin-Franklin boundary area has been visited.

This work owes much to the advice of Dr. R. H. Shevenell, of the Faculty of Arts of the University of Ottawa, to whom grateful thanks are due. The author also wishes to acknowledge the invaluable assistance of Dr. B. Zaborski and T. Jost, Professors of Geography at McGill University and the University of Ottawa, respectively, of Dr. C. C. Lingard of the Canadian Social Science Research Council, of Mr. G. T. Prinsep late of the International Boundary Commission staff, and of Dr. J. W. Watson, as well as the many others who contributed by correspondence or personal comment.

CHAPTER II

THE DEVELOPMENT OF MAJOR POLITICAL BOUNDARIES PRIOR TO 1782

PRE-EUROPEAN PERIOD

Canada was, of course, populated to some extent before its existence was known to Western Europeans. These aboriginal inhabitants had their own political organizations, and although the details are not known in every respect, there is little doubt that boundaries of a sort did exist between some of the tribes. Such boundaries probably arose from the association of a group with a habitat whose food supply was regarded as exclusively its own. Hunting territory divisions were characteristic of the northern Indian tribes of Algonkian stock. These divisions constituted the main bond of union and interest in the families that composed the bands, and all male members shared the right of hunting and fishing within a particular territory. These hunting lands or territories were more or less fixed tracts of country, the boundaries of which were determined by certain rivers, ridges, lakes, or other natural landmarks such as swamps and clumps of trees (163, p. 2).

In southeastern Canada, the boundaries between Indian tribes were principally watersheds. They seem to have been continued seaward to prominent coastal features, along general lines continuing the watersheds. Thus, in what is now New Brunswick, Martins Head on the Bay of Fundy probably separated the Micmacs and Malecites, and Point Lepreau the St. John River Indians from the Passamaquoddies (52, p. 154).

On the northwest coast of British Columbia, the Indians were less migratory and had more sharply defined territorial boundaries. The Haida, Tlinkit, and Tsimshian Indians portioned out all the land on their seaboard villages among the separate families as hunting, fishing, and berrying grounds (151, p. 57). These were regarded as private property and were handed on from generation to generation. If they were used by anyone other than the owner, the privilege had to be paid for. Every salmon stream had its proprietor, whose summer camp would be set up where the run of the fish was greatest. With the Iroquois tribes, tribal property included agricultural land, on which the Indians grew corn, beans, squash, sunflowers, and tobacco, and this agricultural land they divided among the various families.

To the Eskimos, the frozen sea off some promontory often constituted a tribal sealing ground within which poachers would be killed. Even today, boundaries exist between various Eskimo families. By tacit agreement certain areas are regarded as the hunting preserve of one group to the exclusion of all others.

Thus, although boundaries between various population groups did exist, they were generally ill-defined, and varied from time to time, because the lands were not usually held in permanent occupancy and cultivation, as the people relied mainly on hunting and fishing. The pre-European boundaries had little or no effect on the evolution of the major boundary pattern of Canada as it is known today.

PROCLAMATIONS OF SOVEREIGNTY, 1450-1600

The visits to and possible settlements in North America by the Norsemen around 1000 A.D. had even less to do with boundary evolution in Canada than the activities of the aboriginal inhabitants. The first political boundary in North America was established in 1494 by the Treaty of Tordesillas, which

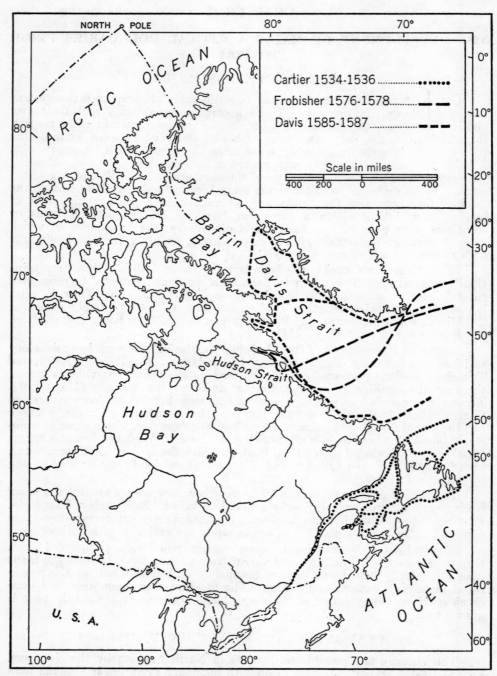

Figure 2. Major voyages of discovery and exploration in eastern Canada before 1600.

delimited the "spheres of influence" of Spain and Portugal. The line agreed upon by the two countries corresponded approximately with the sixtieth meridian west, but it soon fell into desuetude, and left no trace in the present boundary pattern (34, p. 467). Canada began its development with a later period of discovery and exploration that can be characterized as a prelude to successful European settlement. This period began with the "opening" of the Newfoundland fisheries and the voyages of Cabot, Cartier, and Frobisher, and saw the first attempts at colonization.

John Cabot's voyage in 1497 was made under charter from Henry VII of England. This Royal Charter was the first political instrument specifically referring to part of what is now Canada, and resulted, in 1498, in the first formal act of possession relating to the northern part of this continent made by any European power. In that year Cabot claimed all the coast as far south as latitude 34 degrees in the name of the King of England. Similar procedures were probably followed by such men as Corte Real, 1500, for Portugal, Verrazano, 1524, for France, and Gomez, 1524-25, for Spain. Although the voyages resulted in certain claims to general regions, these claims are not perpetuated in any boundary existent today.

The next significant step was taken by Jacques Cartier in 1534. His traditional "first voyage" through the Strait of Belle Isle and the Gulf of St. Lawrence ultimately resulted in his arrival at Gaspe Peninsula, where he set up a wooden cross as a token of his claim to that area for the King of France. His second voyage (1536) extended his discoveries to the sites of the present cities of Quebec and Montreal, and thus to the "land and province" of Canada. His third voyage (1541) made no substantial addition to geographical knowledge.

After Cartier's voyages, the "Canada" that he had discovered and named was the object of no further interest until 1542-53, when the Sieur de Roberval attempted unsuccessfully to form a settlement on the St. Lawrence. Martin Frobisher's voyages in 1576, 1577, and 1578 extended knowledge as far as Baffin Island and Hudson Strait. After Frobisher, Davis made three voyages, in 1585, 1586, and 1587, during which he reached the strait named after him and explored its western shore southward from 66 degrees 40 minutes north.

Meanwhile, Sir Humphrey Gilbert, who had been given a charter in 1578 by Queen Elizabeth, sailed with five ships and two hundred and sixty men to the island of Newfoundland. He established a colony there and proclaimed the sovereignty of his Queen over the island in 1583, but the colony came to a premature end. These were not the first people to live on the island, however, for every part of the east coast was familiar to English fishermen, who were in virtual control at the time of Gilbert's arrival. Gilbert and part of his fleet were lost on the homeward voyage and such men as he left behind joined the fishermen. On January 12, 1598, the Sieur de la Roche was appointed by the King of France as Lieutenant-General of

"Canada, Hochelaga, Newfoundland, Labrador, the River of the Great Bay, of Novembegue, and the lands adjacent to the said provinces and rivers which are the whole length and depth of the country, provided they are not inhabited by the subjects of any other Christian Prince" (123, p. 40).

But the settlements he intended to establish met fates similar to those of Roberval and Gilbert.

A few years before this, in 1592, the Greek explorer, Juan de Fuca, discovered the strait now named for him, on the Pacific coast; the discovery was not significant to Canada's boundary development until a very much later date.

Thus, in 1601, with the beginning of a new century, Canada still awaited settlement. Most of the early activities in the New World were based on the search for a passage to the "Far East", or on the desire for precious metals, and were not fundamentally concerned with settlement. However, "sovereignty" had been proclaimed over large areas of eastern Canada, names had been added to the political map of North America, and the stage had been set for later boundary evolution.

THE BEGINNINGS OF SETTLEMENT, 1600-1763

In 1603, Champlain followed in Cartier's footsteps up the St. Lawrence and beyond to Lachine. The next year, with the Sieur de Monts, he sailed to Acadia under commission from the King of France. The commission sets forth the first precise boundaries assigned by France in the New World as follows:

". . . . pour representer nôtre persone aux païs, territoires, côtes et confins de la Cadie, à commencer dés le quarantiéme degré jusques au quarante-sixiéme; Et en icelle étendue ou partie d'icelle. . . ."[1] (52, p. 158).

These limits, 40 to 46 degrees, were supposed to include the region between Cape Cod and Cape Breton (52, p. 159). De Monts and his expedition explored the Bay of Fundy and the harbour at the mouth of St. John River and then went on to the present St. Croix River, near the mouth of which they spent the winter of 1604-05. In a new voyage in 1608, Champlain founded and named Quebec—the first settlement in Canada that has had an uninterrupted existence to the present day, although long before the founding of Quebec there was a permanent trading post at the mouth of the Saguenay that was probably established by Basque fishermen early in the 16th century (187). During the following years Champlain explored the country in various directions. Among other things, he discovered the lake that bears his name, ascended the Ottawa River, and crossed to Georgian Bay. At his death in 1634, however, New France was little more than an outpost in the wilderness.

Meanwhile, the English had been settling Virginia, the boundaries of which had been fixed by charter of King James I in 1606, allowing the London Company to form settlements between 34 degrees north and 38 degrees north: the Plymouth Company also was allowed to form settlements between 41 degrees and 45 degrees of latitude. It has been suggested that the southern limit of these claims can be traced back to the fact that Cabot reached 34 degrees north in 1497 (93, p. 1). It is also worth noting that it was in the Plymouth Company charter of 1606 that the 45th parallel was mentioned for the first time as a political boundary, although the true genesis of its present use as a political boundary may stem from a Dutch charter of 1614 (111, p. 255).

The boundaries of these British colonies overlapped the French claims, and conflict ensued. But in 1620 King James I gave a new patent to the Plymouth Company that extended their northern boundary to 48 degrees, and included not only the coast region but the interior of the continent as well, in the following terms:

" . . . . all that Circuit, Continent, Precincts, and Limitts, in America, lying and being in Breadth from Fourty Degrees of Northerly Latitude, from the Equnoctiall Line, to Fourty-eight Degrees of the said Northerly Latitude, and in Length by all the Breadth aforesaid, throughout the Maine Land, from Sea to Sea . . . shall be the Limitts, and Bounds and Precincts of the said second Collony . . . ." (52, p. 165).

---

[1] This would appear to be the first occasion on which parallels of latitude were used officially to describe boundaries in Canada.

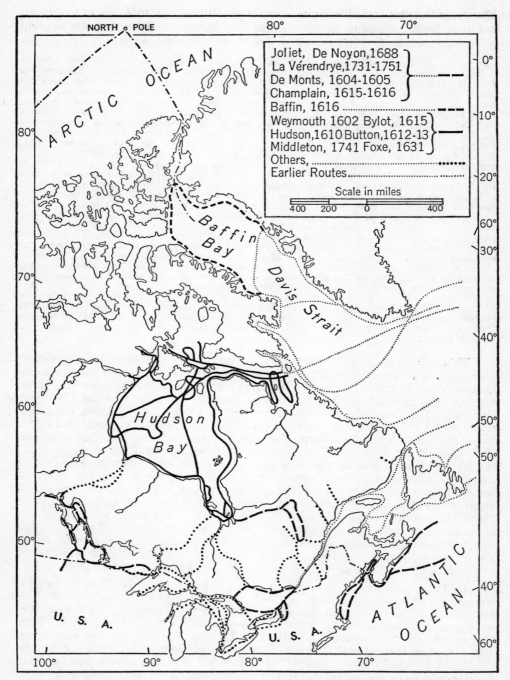

Figure 3. Major voyages of discovery and exploration in eastern Canada between 1600 and 1763.

The extension was probably made in order to establish a British claim to Acadia, but it did not remain in force long, for the next year James I made a grant of Nova Scotia to Sir William Alexander in the following terms:

". . . . all and single, the lands of the Continent and islands situated and lying in America, within the head or promontory commonly called Cape of Sable, lying near the forty-third degree of north latitude, or thereabouts; from this Cape, stretching along the shores of the Sea, westward to the roadstead of St. Mary, commonly called St. Mary's Bay, and thence northward by a straight line, crossing the entrance, or mouth, of that great roadstead Bay of Fundy which runs toward the eastern part of the land between the countries of the Suriqui and Etchimine, commonly called Suriquois and Etchimines. to the river generally known by the name St. Croix, and to the remotest springs, or source, from the western side of the same, which empty into the first mentioned river; thence by an imaginary straight line which is conceived to extend through the land, or run northward to the nearest bay, river, or stream emptying into the great river of Canada; and going from that eastward along the low shores of the same river of Canada to the river, harbour, port, or shore, commonly known and called by the name Gathepe or Gaspie, and thence south-southeast to the isles called Bacalos or Cape Breton, leaving the said isles on the right, and the mouth of the said great river of Canada, or large bay, and the territory of Newfoundland, with the islands belonging to the same lands on the left; thence to the headland, or point of Cape Breton aforesaid, lying near latitude forty-five degrees or thereabouts; and from the said point of Cape Breton toward the south and west to the above mentioned Cape Sable, where the boundary began; including and containing within the said coasts and their circumference, from sea to sea, all lands of the continent with the rivers, falls, bays, shores, islands, or seas, lying near or within six leagues on any side of the same on the west, north or east sides of the same coasts and bounds and on the south-southeast (where Cape Breton lies) and on the south side of the same (where Cape Sable is) all seas and islands southward within forty leagues of said seashore, thereby including the large island commonly called Isle de Sable or Sablon, lying towards Carban, in common speech south-southeast about thirty leagues from the said Cape Breton seaward and being in latitude forty-four Degrees or thereabouts . . ." (13, pp. 105-107).

This delimitation was remarkable in that it was the first national patent that ever was clearly bounded within America by particular and specific geographical features. There were, however, two inconsistencies in these boundaries. First of all they overlapped those of the grants to the Plymouth Company, but this difficulty was easily solved when the Plymouth Company relinquished its claim to the area common with the Alexander grant. Secondly, they, like their other British predecessors, overlapped the boundaries of the area claimed by France. This was particularly important, because, in 1627, the King of France granted a charter to the Company of One Hundred Associates for the development and government of New France, the boundaries of which were defined as extending from Florida to the Arctic Circle, and from Newfoundland on the east to the "great fresh water sea" on the west, including all the "lands in the watershed of the St. Lawrence and its tributaries, and of the other rivers of Canada which flow into the sea, as well as any other lands over which the company may extend the French authority". In 1627 war broke out between the two countries. This temporarily terminated with the Treaty of St. Germain-en-Laye in 1632, which restored all places in Acadia to France.

In 1635 the Council for New England granted Lord William Alexander, son of Sir William Alexander, a tract of land adjacent to that granted to his father in 1621. Despite these events, however, Cromwell, Lord Protector of Great Britain, in 1656, granted most of the present Nova Scotia, New Brunswick, and Prince Edward Island to Thomas Temple and two associates. But a further outbreak of war with France, which terminated with the Treaty of Breda in 1667, also restored to France all Acadia, which had a local Governor responsible to the Governor of Quebec. Intermittent disputes over the interpretation of these treaties occurred between France and Britain, which in 1686 resulted in an agreement between the monarchs of the two countries. This agreement recognized the need for drawing a boundary line between the respective possessions of the two countries in the New World and provided for the settlement of this boundary by a joint commission (150, p. x). But it was never put into effect. Open warfare between the two countries broke out again in 1689. It concluded in 1697 with the Treaty of Ryswick, which again restored the British conquests to France, but the war of 1702-1713, which terminated with the Treaty of Utrecht (1713), resulted in the French surrender of her interests in Nova Scotia (Acadia, but not including Cape Breton Island) and Newfoundland (except for certain fishing rights) to the British. During the negotiations regarding this treaty, reference was made to the boundaries between the French and English areas, but the language of the treaty with regard to them remained vague.

In the meantime, the voyages of Frobisher and Davis in the Hudson Bay area had been followed up. A series of expeditions started by Henry Hudson in 1610 was continued by Sir Thomas Button in 1612 and 1613. Button erected a cross at the mouth of Nelson River and took possession of those parts in the name of Great Britain. Robert Bylot and William Baffin followed in 1615 and 1616, and Captains Foxe and James in 1631, each taking formal possession of the places where he landed. But further political development in this area had to wait for 40 years, until 1670, when Prince Rupert and seventeen associates obtained from King Charles II a charter as the Governor and Company of Adventurers of England trading into Hudson's Bay. The boundaries of the territory over which the Company were to be "true and absolute lords" were defined as follows:

". . . . all these seas, straits, bays, rivers, lakes, creeks and sounds in whatsoever latitude they shall be, that lie within the entrance of the straits, commonly called Hudson's Straits, together with all the lands and territories upon the countries, coasts, and confines of the seas, bays, lakes, rivers, creeks and sounds aforesaid, that are not already actually possessed by or granted to any of our subjects, or possessed by the subjects of any other Christian Prince or State, . . . and that the said lands be . . . called "Rupert's Land" (123, p. 33).

This area has generally been taken to be the entire area draining into Hudson Bay. But the charter went even beyond "Rupert's land". Where their own government ended, the Company were to have the sole right of trade in all the "havens, bays, creeks, rivers, lakes and seas", into which they could find passage from their own area. Their first step was to place trading posts around the shores of Hudson's Bay, and by 1682 these had been established at Rupert River, Albany River, Hayes Island, Port Nelson, and New Severn (1, p. 221).

France disputed the Hudson's Bay Company's claim from the start, particularly because the French missionaries and traders had extended and consolidated Champlain's discoveries, and it was not until the Treaty of Utrecht that France relinquished her claims, although the final treaty did not establish any definite limits between the territory of France and that of the Hudson's Bay Company. Thus at the conclusion of the war of 1702 to 1713, Canada, Cape Breton Island, Labrador, Anticosti Island, and the present Prince Edward Island remained French, but the boundaries between these territories and those of the British to the north and south of them were not precisely delimited and remained a matter of dispute. However, the treaty provided for the appointment of commissioners to settle such disputes, and of the efforts of these commissioners, those concerned with the boundary of the Hudson's Bay Company lands are of greatest significance here. Indeed, the Treaty of Ryswick provided that the question of the ownership of the posts on Hudson's Bay should be left to the decision of a joint Anglo-French commission, but although a commission appointed for this purpose did meet in 1699, it accomplished nothing.

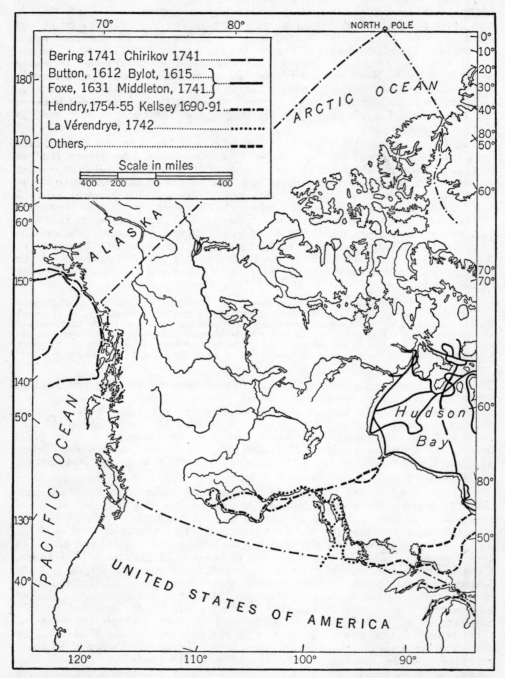

Figure 4. Major voyages of discovery and exploration in western Canada before 1763.

Again, prior to the Treaty of Utrecht, the Hudson's Bay Company stated the terms it wished to have incorporated in the treaty about to be concluded, although this was not done. In 1714, the Company again described its limits as follows:

". . . . and from the said Lake (Mistassini) a Line to Run Southwestward Into 49 Degree North Latitude . . . and that that Latitude be the Limitt . . ." (62, VIII, p. 4068).

This is significant if only for the fact that it is the first official mention of the 49th Parallel in connection with a boundary line. A further proposal followed in 1719, and the British Government instructed the commissioners to obtain the boundary as follows:

"That the same begin from the Island called Grimington's Island or Cape Perdrix in the Latitude of 58½ North . . . further, That a Line be drawn from the South Westward of the Island of Grimington or Cape Perdrix (so as to include the same within the limits of the Bay) to the Great Lake Miscosinke alias Mistosseny, dividing the said Lake into two Parts . . . and that where the said Line shall cut the 49th Degree of Northern Latitude, another Line shall begin and be extended Westward from the said Lake, upon the 49th Degree of Northern Latitude . . ." (150, p. 4).

However, the commissioners accomplished nothing, but various historians and cartographers confused these attempts to settle boundaries with actual settlement, a situation that became significant at a later date.

Between 1713 and 1763, France made a determined effort to secure a firm foothold on the interior of North America. Her missionaries and traders pushed west of the Great Lakes into parts of what is now western Canada. This phase of development was most marked by the work of Daniel de Greysolon, Sieur du Lhut, which began in 1678. It was extended by Jacques de Noyon, who arrived at Lake of the Woods in 1688, and the work of both culminated in the voyages of the Sieur de la Vérendrye and his sons. Between them they crossed what is now southern Manitoba (1731), certainly reached the edge of the Rocky Mountains (1742), and may have penetrated much farther to the westward.

In 1741, war again broke out between France and Britain. It concluded in 1748 with statesmen on both sides realizing that the old boundary question had to be definitely and finally settled. For the next 15 years, three distinct methods were used to bring about a decision (150, pp. 19, 20). The first two—an International Joint Commission and direct diplomacy—failed. The third—open warfare—succeeded, and the years 1756 to 1763 saw the final struggle between France and Britain in North America that was finally resolved by Wolfe's conquest of Quebec.

THE TREATY OF PARIS AND ITS RESULTS

The Treaty of Paris produced the greatest rearrangement of boundaries in North America that had hitherto occurred. It is for this reason that the war that immediately preceded it is sometimes called the "War of the Boundary Lines". France now definitely withdrew from the mainland of North America. She ceded to Britain, Canada, Cape Breton Island, most of the islands in the Gulf of St. Lawrence, all of the then Nova Scotia, and all her former territories east of Mississippi River, except New Orleans, which went to Spain. She also ceded to Spain all her former territory west of Mississippi River from the Gulf of Mexico northwards to the sources of Missouri River, known as Louisiana. Britain gained the Spanish possessions east and southeast of Mississippi River, which included Florida, and thus, at this date, the entire eastern half of the

North American continent was British territory. All boundary questions in this area now became questions between provinces, all under one crown. All that remained to France were the islands of St. Pierre and Miquelon off the coast of Newfoundland.

Having acquired so much new territory, it then became necessary for Britain to provide the machinery by which it could be governed. In that part of the territory that now forms part of Canada, three political areas had existed prior to 1763—Quebec, Newfoundland, and Nova Scotia. These were retained, but the boundaries were more precisely delimited. In the case of Quebec, the precise boundaries presented some problems, for, as early as 1762, the British military governors in Quebec and Montreal had stated that it was impossible to ascertain exactly what part of North America the French styled Canada, although from the trade they carried on it appeared that Canada included all the Great Lakes and the Mississippi basin above the junction of that river with the Illinois (161, p. 96). But to place all this area under one colonial jurisdiction at the close of the war was considered unwise by the British Board of Trade and Plantations. First of all, formal inclusion within Canada might imply that the British title to these lands was the result of the Treaty of Utrecht, whereas it was considered to rest on antecedent rights, an impression the British wished particularly to convey to the Indians. Secondly, if the Indian territory were annexed to one particular province and subjected to its laws, that province would have an unfair advantage over the other provinces with respect to the Indian trade. Thirdly, the laws of the province could not be enforced without establishing military garrisons throughout the area, which, even if it were feasible, might possibly cause friction between the civil and military governors (161, pp. 151, 152).

Finally, it was suggested that the boundaries of Canada should be restricted in order to prevent settlement from spreading too far from established government, trade, and communication (161, p. 141).

Therefore, in 1763, a Royal Proclamation was issued describing the boundaries of Quebec as follows:

". . . . bounded on the Labrador coast by the River St. John, and from thence by a Line drawn from the Head of that River, through the Lake St. John, to the South end of the Lake Nipissim; from whence the said Line, crossing the River St. Lawrence, and the Lake Champlain, in 45 Degrees of North Latitude, passes along the High Lands which divide the Rivers that empty themselves into the said River St. Lawrence from those which fall into the Sea; and also along the North Coast of the Baye des Chaleurs and the Coast of the Gulph of St. Lawrence to Cape Rosieres, and from thence crossing the mouth of the River St. Lawrence by the West End of the Island of Anticosti, terminates at the aforesaid River of St. John" (90, p. 18).

Lake St. John is the source of Saguenay River, whereas Lake Nipissing is connected by French River to Georgian Bay and Lake Huron. From Lake Nipissing the boundary ran to the west of, and parallel with, the Ottawa River until it met the St. Lawrence at the Long Sault Rapids. Thus the "core area" of French settlement was enclosed within the province. Its internal communications were maintained, yet from its borders easy access to the Indian territory and the other British provinces for trading purposes was preserved.

The same Royal Proclamation assigned to the Government of Newfoundland the "coast" of North America from "the River St. John's to Hudson's streights, together with the Islands of Anticosti and Madelaine, and all other smaller islands lying upon the said Coast" (161, p. 164). The purpose of this award to Newfoundland was to allow its fishermen to extend their codfishing operations to the coast of Labrador and the adjacent islands, and the western boundary had been fixed at St. John River[1] in the belief that the French Canadians had no settlements east of it (161, p. 542).

All other parts of the mainland north of the St. Lawrence, not included in Quebec, Newfoundland, or the territory granted to the Hudson's Bay Company, were assigned to the Crown.

The islands of St. John and Cape Breton, or Isle Royale, with the lesser islands adjacent thereto, were annexed to the Government of Nova Scotia.

The boundaries of Nova Scotia were set forth in greater detail in the commission to Montague Wilmot, as Governor of the Province, under date of November 21, 1763, as follows:

". . . . To the northward our said province shall be bounded by the southern boundary of our Province of Quebec, as far as the western extremity of the Baye des Chaleurs, to the eastward by the said Bay and the gulf of St. Lawrence to the Cape or Promontory called Cape Breton in the Island of that name including that Island, the Island of St. John's and all other Islands within six leagues of the coast, to the southward by the Atlantic Ocean from the said Cape to Cape Sable including all other islands, within forty leagues of the coast, with all the rights, members and appurtenances whatever thereunto belonging and to the westward, although our said province hath anciently extended and doth of right extend as far as the River Pentagoet or Penobscot, it shall be bounded by a line drawn from Cape Sable across the entrance of the Bay of Fundy to the mouth of the River St. Croix, by the said river to its source and by a line drawn due north from thence to the southern boundary of our Colony of Quebec" (76, p. 275).

The reasons for this unification of the Maritimes were chiefly to consolidate Great Britain's claims to the area. The part that was later to become New Brunswick had been claimed by Britain as a legal and integral part of Nova Scotia for half a century, although civil government was not established there. With the withdrawal of the French forces, the government of Nova Scotia was able, for the first time, to exercise effective authority there. St. John's Island and Cape Breton Island, which had been expressly granted to France in 1713, now had to be provided with new government. Thus the annexation of these three areas to Nova Scotia was not only the best, but almost the only solution (161, p. 142). It was not a union of colonies, but merely an extension of territorial jurisdiction (194, pp. 41, 42).

BRITISH NORTH AMERICA BEFORE THE REVOLUTION, 1763-1782

From 1763, the territorial expansion of Canada was purely British, and it was from this date that definite political boundaries began to emerge. The emergence of these boundaries was, for the greater part of the period, connected with political developments in the colonies south of Quebec and Nova Scotia.

The Quebec Act 1774 stemmed from such developments, as well as from the need to make some further provision for administration of the country outside the limits of the Quebec of 1763. Eleven years had passed since it had been decided to leave the area west of Quebec as an Indian reserve. It was maintained that the area had become "the theatre of disorder and confusion" (161, p. 542) and the time had now arrived for some recognized law and government to be extended to it (161, p. 485). More was now known about the area; such permanent settlers as it had were French rather than British, and it was obviously better for them to be included with Quebec rather than with any of the purely British colonies. It was also thought that the Indians would be

---

[1] The present Rivière St. Jean.

better cared for under the government of Quebec. Furthermore, the waterways made communication to the west easier from Canada than from the southern colonies. Thus the new southern and western boundaries of Quebec remained as they had been since 1763, as far as the intersection of the 45th parallel with the river. From this point they followed the St. Lawrence and the Great Lakes up to the point on the south shore of Lake Erie where the old French route to the Ohio left it. From this point the boundary ran across country to the Ohio and thence to the Mississippi.

The act also restored Labrador, Anticosti, and the Magdalen Islands to Quebec, and the boundaries of the old province were further defined as extending north to the Hudson's Bay Company's territories. The interval between 1774 and the Royal Proclamation of 1763 had also shown that the French Canadians had a variety of claims upon the coast of Labrador between St. John River and the Strait of Belle Isle. It was discovered that a cod fishery was impracticable off the greater part of the coast and that it could be used only "for that species of sedentary Seal Fishery which is in its nature inconsistent with the Regulations of the Fishery at Newfoundland" (161, p. 542). Consequently, when the Governor of Newfoundland issued a regulation in 1765 forbidding the sedentary fishermen of Quebec to fish on the coast of Labrador, they protested, and the Lords of Trade in London proposed, in 1772, that the southwestern section of the Labrador coast between the River St. John and the Anse des Espagnols should be restored to Quebec. Ultimately, however, it was decided that this partition would be inadequate to protect the interests of the Quebec fishermen, and the whole of Labrador was transferred to their province. The boundary clause of the Quebec Act of 1774 was as follows:

"bounded on the South by a Line from the Bay of Chaleurs, along the High Lands which divide the Rivers that empty themselves into the River Saint Lawrence from those which fall into the Sea, to a Point in Forty-five Degrees of Northern Latitude, on the Eastern Bank of the River Connecticut, keeping the same Latitude directly West, through the Lake Champlain, until, in the same Latitude, it meets the River Saint Lawrence; from thence up the Eastern Bank of the said River to the Lake Ontario; thence through the Lake Ontario, and the River commonly called Niagara; and thence along by the Eastern and South-eastern Bank of Lake Erie, following the said Bank, until the same shall be intersected by the Northern Boundary, granted by the Charter of the Province of Pennsylvania, in case the same shall be so intersected; and from thence along the said Northern and Western Boundaries of the said Province, until the said Western Boundary strike the Ohio: But in case the said Bank of the said Lake shall not be found to be so intersected, then following the said Bank until it shall arrive at that Point of the said Bank which shall be nearest to the North-western Angle of the said Province of Pennsylvania, and thence, by a right Line, to the said North-western Angle of the said Province; and thence along the Western Boundary of the said Province, until it strike the River Ohio; and along the Bank of the said River, Westward, to the Banks of the Mississippi, and Northward to the Southern Boundary of the Territory granted to the Merchants Adventurers of England, trading to Hudson's Bay; and also all such Territories, Islands, and Countries, which have, since the Tenth of February, One Thousand seven hundred and sixty-three, been made Part of the Government of Newfoundland, be, and they are hereby, during His Majesty's Pleasure, annexed to, and made Part and Parcel of, the Province of Quebec" (161, p. 571).

Thus was the contention met that the trade and prosperity of Quebec had suffered from the separation of the upper Indian trading posts and the coast of Labrador from Canada (161, pp. 510, 511). Thus, too, were all the Illinois country and all the western lands for which Britain and France had fought confirmed to Canada.

But it must also be mentioned that a far from minor reason for the westward extension of Quebec was the fact that the southern colonies were on the verge of revolution and that Britain was, therefore, loth to trust them with the Indian territory. Unfortunately, the passage of the Quebec Act was taken as a further provocation by the southern colonies, as they objected to the great extension southward of the boundaries of Quebec, which would interfere with the westward expansion of all the colonies lying north of the 37th parallel (the latitude of the mouth of the Ohio). In 1776, they revolted and declared their independence.

Meanwhile, the expulsion of the Acadians from St. John's Island in 1758, and the withdrawal of the French military forces, had left the island almost deserted. In order to begin to recolonize this territory, the British Government sent a surveyor to the island in 1764. At that time only thirty families were living on the island, in an extremely poor condition. After the survey, the land was granted to absentee proprietors in England, and by 1767 the whole of the island had been disposed of in this manner. However, no sooner had the landlords received their grants from the Governor of Nova Scotia than they felt the necessity for a capital seat within their own territory (109, pp. 343, 344). They petitioned the king for the complete separation of their island from the mainland, stressing the inconvenience of having to refer all judicial and legal matters to Halifax. At the best of times the journey to Halifax was tedious and expensive, and during the winter months it was impracticable because of ice. They also pointed out that the peninsula of Nova Scotia, with settlement projects of its own, could hardly be expected to give energetic support to immigration schemes for the island, and they could hardly have been unmindful of the risk to their own proprietary rights involved in prolonged control by the Halifax legislature with its New England traditions of liberalism (194, pp. 43, 44).

The island was, therefore, separated from Nova Scotia in 1769; it was renamed Prince Edward Island in 1798.

Thus, by 1782, settlement in parts of what is now southern Canada had become firmly established. Proclamations of sovereignty had been made in northern Canada and definite delimitations of territory had been made comprising six divisions—the provinces of Quebec, Nova Scotia, and St. John's Island (Ile St. Jean), the Hudson's Bay Company territories, Newfoundland, and certain lands belonging directly to the Crown. Although these delimitations contained what later proved to be inconsistencies, they had been settled according to the geographical lights of the time, but no attempt was made to demarcate these legal lines on the ground. The American revolution was drawing to a close, foreshadowing boundary changes of even more significance to Canada than those that had preceded it.

CHAPTER III

THE DEVELOPMENT OF MAJOR POLITICAL BOUNDARIES FROM 1782 TO 1866

After 6 years of warfare, negotiations for peace began between Great Britain and the American colonies. These were concluded in 1783 by the Treaty of Paris, following which the United States of America came officially into being. It is from this date that Canada's present southern international boundary began to take more definite shape. Indeed the American revolution had such a profound effect on Canada that it was almost refounded as a result of it.

INTERNATIONAL CONSEQUENCES OF THE AMERICAN REVOLUTION

One effect of the American Revolution was to reverse Great Britain's relative position as it had existed at the time of the Treaty of Ryswick. So far as territorial claims and counter-claims were concerned, Great Britain, after the revolution, occupied France's former position, and the United States Great Britain's. It was natural then that the United States should press for the same boundaries between themselves and Canada as Britain had claimed against the French, and the ultimate result was that Great Britain retained the Quebec, Nova Scotia, and Newfoundland of 1763, but lost the Illinois country and the lands south and west of the Great Lakes that had been included in Quebec by the Act of 1774. The original limits between the United States and British territory were first definitely described in the provisional treaty of November 30, 1782, and the definitive treaty of peace, concluded September 3, 1783, defined them in similar terms as follows:

". . . . from the North-west Angle of Nova Scotia, viz., that Angle which is formed by a line drawn due North, from the source of St. Croix River to the Highlands, along the said Highlands which divide those Rivers that empty themselves into the River St. Lawrence from those which fall into the Atlantic Ocean, to the North-westernmost head of Connecticut River; thence down along the middle of that River to the 45th degree of North latitude; from whence by a line due West on said latitude until it strikes the River Iroquois or Cataraquy[1]; thence along the middle of the said River into Lake Ontario; through the middle of said Lake until it strikes the communication by water between that Lake and Lake Erie; thence along the middle of said communication into Lake Erie; through the middle of said Lake until it arrives at the water-communication between that Lake and Lake Huron; thence along the middle of said water-communication into the Lake Huron; thence through the middle of said Lake to the water-communication between that Lake and Lake Superior; thence through Lake Superior, Northward of the Isles Royal and Phelipeaux, to the Long Lake[2]; thence through the middle of said Long Lake, and the water-communication between it and the Lake of the Woods, to the said Lake of the Woods; thence through the said Lake to the most North-western point thereof, and from thence on a due West course to the River Mississippi; thence by a line to be drawn along the middle of the said River Mississippi, until it shall intersect the Northmost part of the 31st degree of North latitude; South by a line to be drawn due East from the determination of the line last mentioned, in the latitude of 31 degrees North of the Equator, to the middle of the River Apalachicola or Catahouche; thence along the middle thereof to its junction with the Flint River; thence straight to the head of St. Mary's River, and thence down along the middle of St. Mary's River to the Atlantic Ocean: East by a line to be drawn along the middle of the River St. Croix, from its mouth in the Bay of Fundy to its source; and from its source directly North to the aforesaid Highlands, which

---

[1] The present St. Lawrence River.
[2] The present Rainy Lake.

divide the Rivers that fall into the Atlantic Ocean from those which fall into the River St. Lawrence: comprehending all Islands within 20 leagues of any part of the shores of The United States, and lying between lines to be drawn due East from the points where the aforesaid Boundaries between Nova Scotia on the one part, and East Florida on the other, shall respectively touch the Bay of Fundy, and the Atlantic Ocean; excepting such Islands as now are, or heretofore have been, within the limits of the said Province of Nova Scotia" (161, pp. 727-28).

After the usual compromises between the two sides had been agreed upon, the precise location of the boundary was probably based on the application to the existing maps of the time of principles previously adopted. The idea of dividing each of the Great Lakes (except Michigan) into two parts had first appeared in the Quebec Act of 1774, and it must have appeared logical to extend the lake boundary to the western shore of Lake Superior. The boundary farther westward must also have appeared to be a logical extension of the river-lake line, particularly as the map the negotiators had before them was one made by John Mitchell in 1755 that showed Lake of the Woods and its water connection with Lake Superior. However, in deciding upon this section of the boundary, the British negotiators overlooked the fact that in agreeing that the United States should have Grand Portage they were dealing a severe blow to the Canadian fur trade. This portage route was of the greatest economic importance to Canada, for by it passed the goods of the Montreal fur merchants en route to the western territory and down it came furs worth £200,000 a year. The new boundary prevented the use of this route, as the topography of the country on the north or British bank of the river made a portage there impossible. The North West Company, therefore, employed two men to search for another route from Lake Superior to Lake Winnipeg entirely within British territory. They found a canoe route from Lake Superior by way of Lake Nipigon, Sturgeon Lake, and English River to Portage de l'Isle on Winnipeg River (19, p. 336), but this route was so inconvenient and difficult that it was never adopted by the traders. Furthermore, owing to disputes between the British and United States governments regarding the implementation of some of the terms of the treaty of 1783, the Grand Portage route continued to be used by the Canadians for another 17 or 18 years. When finally compelled to abandon it, the traders used the Kaministiquia route, which had, fortunately, been "rediscovered" in 1798. Only a few miles north of the new international boundary, it had been used by the French traders before 1763 and then forgotten.

In any case, by this time, other controversial points about the boundary had come to a head. Mitchell's map was so inaccurate that at least nine distinct boundary problems arose (10, p. 42). The Treaty of London, 1794 (Jay's Treaty), began the process of clarifying these. Among other things, the treaty also provided for the protection of the fur trade and the security of the Grand Portage route by permitting the free passage of both traders and goods across the portage on both sides of the boundary (5, p. 477).

Under the fifth article of this treaty, commissioners were appointed to deal with another of these problems. They were asked to determine exactly what river was truly intended under the name of the River St. Croix in the Treaty of Peace of 1783. This had become an acute problem when Nova Scotia proceeded to grant land on the eastern bank of Schoodic River to Loyalist refugees from the United States, and Massachusetts requested the Governor of Nova Scotia to recall "those subjects of His Majesty" who had settled in what he considered to be Massachusetts. Excavations at the mouth of the Schoodic disclosed the remains of the Sieur de Mont's winter camp of 1604 and conclusively identified it as the St. Croix of Champlain (31, p. 590); the commissioners decided accordingly on October 25, 1798.

INTERNAL CONSEQUENCES OF THE AMERICAN REVOLUTION

The independence of the United States affected Canadian boundaries in other ways also. In all cases, however, the ultimate cause of the change was due to the fact that, at the close of the Revolutionary War, thousands of Loyalists moved into what remained of British North America. Naturally they took up lands in those areas that had hitherto been unsettled.

In Nova Scotia, these lands were mainly in the St. John Valley and along the north shore of the Bay of Fundy, and it was to these areas that most of the Loyalists went in eastern Canada. This sudden advent of thousands of immigrants, many of whom were destitute, created judicial and administrative problems with which the government of Halifax was unable to deal adequately, particularly as it had equally urgent problems nearer home owing to immigration to various parts of its peninsular territory. The apparent neglect by the authorities in Halifax and the delays in the issue of land patents only accentuated the inconvenience that had been felt before the Loyalist influx, owing to the fact that the remoter parts of the province lacked courts and land offices and also an adequate voice in the Assembly (194, p. 45). Consequently, in 1784, New Brunswick was established as a separate colony, the division being made from Cumberland Arm of the Bay of Fundy across the Chignecto Isthmus to Baie Verte. However, as strong a motive for this decision was the "divide and rule" policy of the British authorities. With the experience of the American revolution fresh in their minds, they took the view that small, separate colonies would show less independence than large ones. "The object. . . . was to govern by means of division, to break them down as much as possible into petty isolated communities, incapable of combination, and possessing no sufficient strength for individual resistance to the Empire" (54, p. 391). Indeed, the British government must have been particularly satisfied at seeing a separate Loyalist government erected between the New England states and peninsular Nova Scotia, whose conduct during the revolution had been "under considerable suspicion" (194, p. 46). This was hardly surprising, as on the eve of the Revolution more than half the population was classified as American. The British Under Secretary of State for the Colonies had even suggested the creation of another province between New Brunswick and Maine (23, p. 272).

About 3,000 Loyalists went to Cape Breton Island—a relatively small number. After the peace of 1763, no grants of lands were made on the island, in order to prevent monopolies and encourage the fisheries, as the French had done. Licences to occupy fishing lots were issued, but no other legal title. This situation continued, at first, to apply to Loyalists after the American Revolution. They could obtain free grants and other allowances in the rest of Nova Scotia but not on Cape Breton Island. Consequently, most of them followed the majority of the older inhabitants in the exploitation of the fisheries (194, p. 47). Owing to these unique conditions, as there were no absolute titles to land, the inhabitants were not freeholders and could not send representatives to a constitutional assembly. Consequently, special legislation had to be drafted for Cape Breton, and it was, therefore, separated from Nova Scotia in 1784.

In Quebec, most of the unsettled lands were southwest of the Ottawa River and along the north shores of Lakes Erie and Ontario. Before 1763, as has been pointed out, the French did considerable exploration, not only in what is now Canada but also in the whole of North America. Apart from long overland journeys such as those of the La Vérendryes, they explored intensively the area about the Great Lakes. But their areas of *settlement* never extended much farther west than Montreal. Indeed, it was not until after the signing of the peace treaty between the French and the Iroquois in 1700, which removed the threat of Indian aggression, that the land northwest and west of Montreal was cleared and settled. This area was first divided in 1702, when two seigniories were granted to Pierre Joybert de Soulanges and Philippe Rigaud de Vaudreuil; the seigniories of Rigaud and Nouvelle Longueuil were added in 1732 and 1734 respectively. Land clearance and settlement proceeded very slowly until 1763, however, when a more determined effort was made to find settlers at "the eleventh hour of the French dominion" (145, p. 129).

In the Ottawa Valley, although a pioneer farmer had cleared land near Chats Falls in 1776, little other settlement occurred before 1796. Only one grant of land had been made during the French régime in what is today the Ontario part of the valley, when the seigniory of Pointe à l'Orignal was granted to François Provost in 1674. It extended along the south shore of Ottawa River for 6 miles, and inland for 6 miles, and with the grant went the right to fish, hunt, trade with the Indians, and exploit any minerals found within its limits (146, pp. 142, 143). Today the area is occupied by the township of Longueuil, named after the family to which the seigniory eventually passed. It was their intention to colonize it, but the first concession was not granted until February 24, 1791, and by 1792 it had only four inhabitants.

In the extreme southwest of the province, settlement was associated with the post established after 1701 by the French at Detroit on the north bank of Detroit River. The colony grew, and by 1752 the area for several miles on both sides of the river was laid out in the typical river-front farms of the French Canadians (144, p. 107). A few British settlers joined them after 1763, and there was a slight increase after 1783 owing to the development of the fur trade.

Thus the majority of the 10,000 Loyalists who had settled between Detroit River and Montreal were west of the Cedars and Coteau rapids on the St. Lawrence below Lake St. Francis, and between the lands granted in seigniory (161, p. 957) and the small settlement near what is now Windsor. The French feudal system of land tenure was contrary to the ideas of these Loyalists, who held their land in free and common socage and they also resented the absence of popular government to which they had been accustomed in the former colonies that were now part of the United States. Some 1,300 Loyalists had settled around Cataraqui, on the site of the present Kingston, and in 1785 a petition was presented on behalf of the new settlers asking for the creation of a district distinct from the province of Quebec whose capital should be Cataraqui and that the "blessings of the British Laws . . . and an exemption from the (French) tenures . . . be extended to the settlement". It also drew attention to the delay in the administration of justice while the area remained part of Quebec "the distance from Detroit to Montreal being not less than Six Hundred Miles, without any Road whatsoever, and the water communication exceedingly tedious, precarious, and during the winter season, absolutely impassable" (161, p. 773). Many similar petitions followed this and ultimately the British government took definite steps to divide the province of Quebec at the boundary of the seigniory granted to De Longueuil (161, p. 957). So far as the settlers near Detroit were concerned, it was the opinion of Dorchester, the Governor of Quebec, that they would not choose to migrate to the lower part of the province even if good land was offered to them. If they did move it would be "attended with much inconvenience, as would their being left insulated and attached to the district of Montreal". He, therefore, merely advised that care should be taken to secure their property and civil rights (161, p. 957). The Constitutional Act of 1791 merely declared the Royal intention to divide the province of Quebec into two separate provinces to be called Upper Canada and Lower

Canada. Precise boundaries were not mentioned because of the difficulty of describing the boundaries between the two provinces and the United States, which depended upon the clarification of certain matters arising from the Treaty of Paris of 1783 (161, p. 1025). The interprovincial boundary was ultimately described by an ~~Order-in-Council dated August 24, 1791~~, as follows:
Proclamation dated November 18, 1791

"To commence at a stone boundary on the north bank of the Lake St. Francis, at the cove west of Pointe au Bodet, in the limit between the township of Lancaster, and the seigneurie of New Longueuil, running along the said limit in the direction of North, thirty-four degrees west, to the westernmost angle of the said seigneurie of New Longueuil, thence along the north western boundary of the seigneurie of Vaudreuil running north twenty five degrees east, until it strikes the Ottawas River, to ascend the said River into the lake Temiscaming, and from the head of the said lake by a line drawn due north until it strikes the boundary line of Hudson's bay, including all the territory to the westward and southward of the said line to the utmost extent of the country commonly called or known by the name of Canada" (161, p. 960).

A more detailed description had been included in the second draft of the Constitutional Bill as follows:

". . . a partition line of various courses running due South from a Stone boundary fixed on the north bank of the Lake Saint Francis in a cove of the River of Saint Lawrence, West of Point au Boudet in the limit between the Township of Lancaster and the seigniory of New Longueuil to the Southernmost extent of His Majesty's Dominions and running in a Northerly direction from the aforesaid stone boundary along the Western or inland bounds of the said Seigniory of New Longueuil and of the Seigniory of Vaudreuil, according to their various courses, until it strikes the Uttawas River, thence in a direct Line to the nearest point in the centre of the navigable channel of the said river, thence ascending the middle of the navigable Channel of the said river to the Lake Temiscaming, thence through the middle of the said Lake to the most Northerly extremity thereof, and thence running due North, to the boundary of the Territory granted to the Merchants Adventurers of England trading to Hudson's Bay" (161, p. 1006).

The main difference between the provisional clause and the one ultimately adopted is that the former made some attempt to indicate that the boundary needed to run south of Pointe au Bodet as well as north, and that it should also divide the *navigable* channel of Ottawa River between the two provinces.

Both descriptions were later found to be faulty, and a note to this effect appears on the plan of part of the Province of Lower Canada made by order of Lord Dorchester in 1794 and 1795. The first error was due to the use of the name "Seigneurie of Vaudreuil" instead of "Seigneurie of Rigaud". The latter had sometimes been referred to by the former name but it led to confusion as there was another Seigniory of Vaudreuil to the east of Rigaud. The northern part of this section of the boundary was obviously intended to follow the western limits of the Seigniory of Rigaud. Secondly, the directions that the boundary was to follow, according to the Royal Proclamation, were not precisely the directions the boundaries of the seigniories actually followed. The western limits of New Longueuil had an actual bearing of N.37°W., not N.34°W., and Rigaud N.19°30'E., not N.25°E. (47, p. 4).

Thus, setting apart the Canadians of French descent with their own government enabled them to preserve their own laws and customs without conflict with the new Canadians of American and British descent who had settled in Upper Canada and established a different set of institutions. The "triangle" between the Ottawa and St. Lawrence Rivers was accordingly included in the Province of Lower Canada, but this area, from the point of view of regional geography, is properly part of the Montreal plain (9, p. 248) and the boundary, therefore, was not merely a line dividing people of different national origins. So far as the anomaly of the Seignory of L'Orignal is concerned, De Longueuil advertised the property for sale in 1784, so that his decision to dispose of his rights may not have been a result of the impending boundary decision. However, by 1796, when he finally succeeded in finding a buyer, the boundary decision had been made, and undoubtedly strengthened his wish to leave a province that was essentially British (29). His land went to an immigrant from the United States named Nathaniel Treadwell and in 1797 L'Orignal village was founded by English-speaking settlers.

Newfoundland and the fisheries in the Gulf of St. Lawrence were also affected by the American revolution, despite their apparent remoteness from the American-Canadian frontier. The people of New England regarded the North Atlantic fisheries as vital to their prosperity, and their fishermen had been accustomed, as British subjects, to conducting their operations off the coast of Labrador and the island of Newfoundland. By the treaty of 1783 they retained this right, but were forbidden to dry or cure fish on the island. Drying and curing was, however, permitted in "any of the unsettled Bays, Harbours and Creeks of Nova Scotia[1], Magdalen Islands, and Labrador, so long as the same shall remain unsettled" (161, p. 728). So far as Labrador and the coasts of the St. Lawrence estuary were concerned, this added to the problems of the government at Quebec. Indeed it was said that there was "no government on the coast" of Labrador (62, p. 1194), and in the Baie de Chaleur area there were "many inconveniences prejudicial to the due management of the said Fisheries . . . from the want of a regular and competent Government" (161, p. 1017). The latter was partly accounted for by the lack of a precisely described southern boundary for Quebec in the Quebec Act of 1774, and attention was given to it prior to the Constitutional Act of 1791. It was even suggested that the fishing settlements in Gaspe might, with advantage, be annexed to New Brunswick, particularly in view of their distance from Quebec city (161, p. 989). But, in spite of the distance, Gaspe was easier to reach from Quebec than St. John's and its commercial ties with Quebec were also much stronger. This would also appear to have been true of the Magdalen Islands, for in 1809 they were confirmed by the Newfoundland Act as being under Quebec jurisdiction. This Act, however, transferred to Newfoundland the coast of Labrador from the River St. John to Hudson Strait, Anticosti Island, and all other smaller islands that had been annexed to it by the Royal Proclamation of 1763 (62, p. 195).

DEVELOPMENTS IN THE WEST

Meanwhile, after a lapse of over 150 years following Juan de Fuca's discoveries, exploration had been taking place along the Pacific coast of North America. The Russians, Bering and Chirikov, had initiated the activity in 1741, and were followed by a number of Spanish explorers working from their post established in 1770 at Monterey. In 1778, Captain Cook explored the Pacific coast from 43 degrees north to 70 degrees north and claimed the northwest coast of America for Great Britain. La Pérouse, the French explorer, supplemented the work of the Russians, Spaniards, and British along the coast in 1786. These discoveries led to great interest in the area by many nations. Eventually, the Spaniards clashed with the British, and when they seized the British post at Nootka Sound an expedition under Captain George Vancouver was dispatched from England. Vancouver's extensive voyages continued from 1792 to 1794. He took formal possession of all the coast from 45 degrees north

---

[1] Which then included the present provinces of Nova Scotia, New Brunswick, and Prince Edward Island.

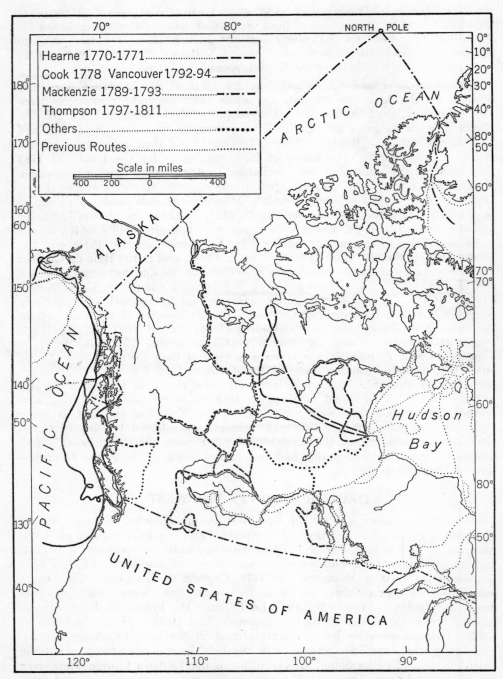

Figure 5. Major voyages of discovery and exploration in western Canada between 1763 and 1814.

to Cape Spencer and divided it into five parts. He named each of his divisions, but made no attempt to give them eastern limits, and as they had little influence on later boundary development their boundaries are mainly of historical importance (82, p. 265).

On land, the North West Company, which had been formed in 1783, and the Hudson's Bay Company were exploring and exploiting the Pacific and Arctic regions north of Columbia River. Although the Hudson's Bay Company had been established primarily as a trading company, it was also to promote discovery. Many of the exploratory journeys, however, were almost accidental, arising as they did largely from the fur trade. The earliest was that of Henry Kellsey, 1691-92. It is impossible to reconstruct the course of his journey accurately, but he was one of the first men, if not the first, to explore any part of the Canadian northwest. Hendry, in 1754-55 may have reached 114 degrees west. Some of the most important of the early exploratory journeys were made by Samuel Hearne, particularly that of 1769-71, when he reached the Arctic Ocean at the mouth of Coppermine River. In 1789, Alexander Mackenzie descended the river later named for him, and on another remarkable journey, in 1793, reached the Pacific Ocean. He thus showed that the Atlantic and Pacific coasts of Canada could be connected by overland routes, and showed the possibility of obtaining complete control of the fur trade of North America, from 48 degrees north to the Pole, with the exception of the Russian area. "To this", he said, "might be added the fishing in both seas and the markets of the four quarters of the globe" (106, p. 358).

Thus the end of the century saw a controversial but none the less described boundary between the British territory that was to become Canada and the United States. It also saw the rearrangement of provincial boundaries in the eastern part of British North America, and the beginning of its political development in the West. Academic though Vancouver's boundaries are, one cannot help but notice, in his use of parallels of latitude, the similarity between them and the earliest boundaries on the east coast.

The first major change of the century relating to boundaries occurred in 1811, when Lord Selkirk was granted 116,000 square miles of territory by the Hudson's Bay Company (Figure 17). The area was intended for settlement, and comprised the Red River Valley, bounded as follows:

"Beginning on the western shore of Lake Winnipic, at a point in fifty-two degrees and thirty minutes north latitude; and thence running due west to Lake Winipigashish, otherwise called Little Winnipic; then in a southerly direction through the said lake, so as to strike its western shore in latitude fifty-two degrees; then due west to the place where the parallel of fifty-two degrees north latitude intersects the western branch of the Red River, otherwise called Assiniboine; then due south from that point of intersection to the height of land which separates the waters running into Hudson's Bay from those of the Missouri and Mississippi Rivers; then in an easterly direction along the height of land to the source of the River Winnipic (meaning by such last-named river the principal branch of the waters which unite in the Lake Saginagas); thence along the main stream of those waters and the middle of the several lakes through which they pass, to the mouth of the Winnipic River; and thence in a northerly direction through the middle of Lake Winnipic, to the place of beginning: which territory is called Assiniboia. . ." (123, p. 28).

In spite of the confusion that still existed as to the exact location of the boundary between Lake Superior and Lake of the Woods, it is clear that part of the area included within the boundaries of the Selkirk grant lay within United States territory, and the grant was, therefore, inoperative to that extent. A year later, however, war broke out between Great Britain and the United States, and our attention must once more turn to the international scene.

FURTHER DEVELOPMENT OF INTERNATIONAL BOUNDARIES

Louisiana, which had been ceded by France to Spain by the Treaty of Paris in 1763, had been returned to France in 1800. In 1803 France sold the territory to the United States of America, and this purchase raised the question of the precise boundary between the United States and British North America from Lake Superior to the Pacific Ocean.

It will be recalled that by the Treaty of Paris, 1763, the boundary between British North America and United States territory was from the northwest angle of Lake of the Woods westward to the sources of the Mississippi River. This, in itself, was geographically impossible because the Mississippi rises well to the south of the latitude of Lake of the Woods, a fact that appears to have been common knowledge among the fur traders of the time and was shown with reasonable accuracy on many maps drawn before 1782. The official negotiators, however, were ignorant of this. They relied upon the Mitchell map of 1755, the northwest corner of which was unfortunately taken up with an inset so that the sources of the Mississippi could not be shown; these, according to the legend, were not yet known but were "supposed to arise about the 50th degree of latitude and western bounds of this map".

This situation, and the vague northern and western boundaries of the Louisiana Territory, raised the subject of the whole southwestern boundary of Canada, but before these two boundary matters were settled the disputants were involved in the War of 1812. Under the Treaty of Ghent (1814), which brought an end to hostilities, the opportunity was taken to provide for a final adjustment of all outstanding matters of dispute and controversy that had risen from the boundaries as described in the treaty of 1783. As a result of the new treaty four commissions were set up, two of which reached definite conclusions, the other two leaving questions still in doubt. In 1818 this was followed by a convention between Great Britain and the United States that extended the International Boundary westward along the 49th Parallel to the "Stony" (Rocky) Mountains in the following terms:

"It is agreed that a Line drawn from the most North Western Point of the Lake of the Woods, along the forty ninth parallel of North Latitude, or, if the said point shall not be in the Forty ninth Parallel of North Latitude, then that a Line drawn from the said Point due North or South, as the Case may be, until the said Line shall intersect the said Parallel of North Latitude, and from the Point of such Intersection due West along and with the said Parallel shall be the Line of Demarkation between the Territories of the United States, and those of His Britannic Majesty, and that the said Line shall form the Northern Boundary of the said Territories of the United States, and the Southern Boundary of the Territories of His Britannic Majesty, from the Lake of the Woods to the Stony Mountains" (79, p. 187).

The early use of the 49th Parallel as a boundary has already been mentioned. Claimed by the Hudson's Bay Company in 1714-19 as the southern limit of their territory, it had become so frequently marked on maps that when the United States purchased the Louisiana Territory from France, the 49th Parallel was assumed by them to be its northern boundary and was eventually accepted by the negotiators of the 1818 Convention. As both the Louisiana Territory and the Hudson's Bay Company's territory had been described according to drainage basins, no single parallel of latitude could satisfactorily separate them. However, there is a rough coincidence between the Hudson Bay-Gulf of Mexico divide and the 49th Parallel, and although the height of land between the two drainage basins is no mountain range, along much of its course it is marked by groups of low hills (87, p. 361). If one parallel of latitude had to be selected there could have been worse choices than the forty-ninth.

Obviously this boundary crossed the southern part of the Selkirk grant, and the Selkirk Estate was, therefore, obliged to relinquish its claim to the area south of the 49th Parallel, which became absorbed into the Dakotas and Minnesota. In the 7 years between the time the grant was made to Selkirk and the extension of the International Boundary to the Rocky Mountains, settlement as far south of Fort Garry (Winnipeg) as 49 degrees north, was very sparse. However, in the very year that the International Boundary extension was agreed upon, a party of French Canadians from Lower Canada settled in the neighbourhood of Pembina with the intention of farming. There they were joined by half-breeds and hunters; houses were built and a church erected. This settlement was probably established under the impression that it was in British territory, but in 1822 doubts about this arose and most of the settlers were persuaded to move farther north and the Hudson's Bay Company's fort (Fort Daer) was abandoned. In the following year observations by American authorities showed that the whole of the settlement of Pembina with the exception of a single log house was within the United States. "About 350 people, two-thirds half-breeds, the rest Swiss and Scotch, preferred to remain at Pembina under the protection of the United States government" (110, p. 28).

Thus, by 1822, the Selkirk settlement had been mainly confined to the area north of the 49th Parallel. Actually, one Hudson's Bay Post north of Pembina remained on United States soil until 1876, connected by wagon road to Fort Garry (89, p. 242); for the movement of local trade had always been influenced by regional rather than political forces and this long continued in the face of merely political considerations (129, p. 231).

The situation with regard to the area west of the Rocky Mountains was covered by Article III of the 1818 Convention. According to its terms, the area was to be "free and open" to the "vessels, citizens and subjects" of both Great Britain and the United States for a period of 10 years without prejudice to the claims of either side (49, p. 13).

This Article was inserted simply because traders of both countries were active in the area. In fact, three countries were by now involved in the whole of the Pacific Northwest. Great Britain, by virtue of the activities of Cook, Vancouver, and the Hudson's Bay and North West Companies (which joined forces in 1821); the United States, especially after 1819 when, by the Treaty of Florida Blanca, Spain ceded to the United States all her rights and claims north of latitude 42 degrees north; and Russia.

The first Russian settlement in the area had been established in 1784 on Kodiak Island. This was followed by several others along the Pacific coast of North America, particularly after 1799, when Russia granted the Russian-American Company exclusive trading privileges north of the 65th parallel.

In 1821, Alexander I of Russia issued a Ukase granting rights of "commerce, whaling and fishing, and of all other industry" on the North American coast between Bering Strait and latitude 51 degrees north to Russian subjects exclusively and prohibiting foreigners from approaching the coast within 100 miles. The United States protested against this, denying in toto the Russian claim south of latitude 55 degrees north and asserting some claim to the coasts as far as 61 degrees north. Great Britain also objected, as she claimed the coast to approximately 58 degrees north (31, p. 596), the northern boundary of Vancouver's "New Norfolk".

The conflicting interests of Russia, the United States, and Great Britain in this area were partly resolved by treaty. In 1824, by a convention between Russia and the United States, the former renounced all claims to territory south of 54 degrees 40 minutes north, and in 1825 Russia and Great Britain reached an agreement on the boundary between their respective territories, which became known as the Alaska boundary.

In the negotiations over this boundary, the Russian Government was guided by the representations of the Russian-American Company and the British Government by those of the Hudson's Bay Company. The boundary the negotiators were seeking to define was thus very largely the boundary between the areas of operations of these companies.

The Russians were particularly interested in retaining control of the Pacific coast of North America north of 55 degrees north, which was the southern limit mentioned in the trading charter of 1799. Their most southern and easterly settlement in 1821 was at Sitka. Great Britain, however, was anxious that the territory that she claimed in the interior should not be shut in by a coastal strip controlled by another power. The Hudson's Bay and North West Companies certainly had no posts on the Pacific coast betwen the 51st and 60th parallels, but it was recognized by both parties that the Mackenzie River area was within their jurisdiction. In the first informal stages of the negotiations, Great Britain proposed Cross Sound and Lynn Canal, at approximately 58 degrees north, as the boundary on the coast, and a due north line from the head of Lynn Canal at approximately 135 degrees west, as the boundary on the mainland. The Russians proposed 54 degrees north as the coastal boundary and whatever longitude would leave Mackenzie River on the British side of the frontier.

The Russians insisted that the southeastern part of the boundary should be a line roughly paralleling the coast at some distance inland, but the farther south and east the Russian demands went, the farther westward did the British push the meridional boundary. At successive stages of the negotiations, the 139th, 140th, and 141st meridians were all mentioned. Ultimately, the 141st meridian was selected as the boundary, probably because it was the line running north from Mount St. Elias. This was one of the few outstanding and unmistakable features in a relatively unknown land, and so supplied a point of reference for both the northern part of the boundary and the southeastern part. Throughout the negotiations, however, the land boundary was really secondary to the question of the extent of Russia's maritime jurisdiction, and, therefore, the shifting of the land boundary a few miles in one direction or the other was not regarded as of great importance by either nation (74, p. 206). Articles III and IV of the treaty of February 28, 1825, defined the line of delimitation between the Russian-British territory as follows:

"III . . . . Commencing from the southernmost point of the island called Prince of Wales Island, which point lies in the parallel of 54 degrees 40 minutes, north latitude, and between the 131st and 133rd degree of west longitude (meridian of Greenwich), the said line shall ascend to the north along the channel called Portland Channel, as far as the point of the continent where it strikes the 56th degree of north latitude; from this last mentioned point, the line of demarcation shall follow the summit of the mountain situated parallel to the coast as far as the point of intersection of the 141st degree of west longitude (of the same meridian); and, finally, from the said point of intersection, the said meridian line of the 141st degree, in its prolongation as far as the Frozen Ocean, shall form the limit between the Russian and British possessions on the continent of America to the north-west.

IV. With reference to the line of demarcation laid down in the preceding Article it is understood:

1st. That the island called Prince of Wales Island shall belong wholly to Russia.

2nd. That whenever the summit of the mountains which extend in a direction parallel to the coast, from the 56th degree of north latitude to the point of intersection of the 141st degree of west longitude, shall prove to be at the distance of more than 10 marine leagues from the ocean, the limit between the British possessions and the line of coast which is to belong to Russia, as above mentioned, shall be formed by a line parallel to the windings of the coast, and which shall never exceed the distance of 10 marine leagues therefrom" (74, p. 203).

The boundary between British territory and the United States, however, remained unsettled until the Oregon Treaty of 1846. The arrangement made for joint occupation in 1818 had been extended in 1827 for an indefinite period. As early as 1824, the British government had offered a boundary that followed the 49th Parallel westward to Columbia River and then followed that river to its mouth. The United States, however, insisted on an extension of the 49th Parallel to the Pacific Ocean. They repeated their proposal in 1826, contending that they needed the safe, commodious harbours of Puget Sound rather than the dangerous entrance to Columbia River, which the British proposal would have left them. The Americans also put forward the principle of contiguity, claiming that the acceptance of the 49th Parallel as a boundary east of the Rocky Mountains established their right to the prolongation of the boundary westward along that parallel (72, p. 124).

In the meantime, the Hudson's Bay Company had been exploring, exploiting, and consolidating the areas between Russian territory and the 49th Parallel, and in 1841 the Governor of the Company approved the choice of a new site for Fort Vancouver because he had come to the conclusion that when the International Boundary was fixed it should go through Juan de Fuca Strait (143, p. 283). But by 1846 American immigration into the Oregon area had increased to such an extent that there were 700 American settlers there as against 400 British, although there were only 8 American settlers north of Columbia River when the Oregon dispute entered its final stage (114, p. 683). In 1844, negotiations between Britain and America began again. The British repeated their offer of 1824 with a free port or ports. The United States declined and, despite President Polk's pre-election cry of "Fifty-four Forty or Fight", which was based on the 1824 convention with Russia, ultimately repeated their proposal of 1826, with a free port or ports on Vancouver Island. This the British rejected, but finally proposed the 49th Parallel, reserving the whole of Vancouver Island. The United States agreed to this and the boundary extension was described as follows:

"From the point on the forty-ninth parallel of north latitude where the boundary laid down in existing treaties and conventions between the United States and Great Britain terminates, the line of boundary between the territories of the United States and those of Her Britannic Majesty shall be continued westward along the said forty-ninth parallel of north latitude to the middle of the channel which separates the continent from Vancouver's Island; and thence southerly through the middle of the said channel, and of Fuca's Straits to the Pacific Ocean: provided, however, that the navigation of the whole of the said channel and Straits, south of the forty-ninth parallel of north latitude remain free and open to both Parties" (79, p. 191).

Thus, after rejecting the 49th Parallel four times, the British government proposed it in 1846! It has been suggested that the reasons for this apparent "about face" were that, by 1846, Columbia River was not so essential to the trade of the Hudson's Bay Company as it had previously insisted, and also that the British government was not especially interested in or concerned with Oregon, particularly if it was going to involve it in war (113, pp. 653-77). In these circumstances, the parallel was probably chosen because it had been suggested by the United States in 1818, and also because it was a convenient extension of a boundary already agreed upon, and bisected the area in dispute.

FURTHER ADJUSTMENTS IN THE EAST

Meanwhile, in the east, still further boundary adjustment had been taking place between the British Colonies. In 1820, Cape Breton Island was re-annexed to Nova Scotia. It will be recalled that its separation in 1784 stemmed from the intention to reserve the island as a headquarters for the fisheries and for the working of the mines. But, in the meantime, a survey of the island for colonization purposes had been completed and grants of land had been authorized. Gradually, therefore, through immigration and settlement, the number of inhabitants entitled to vote increased, so that by 1820 the situation of 1783 no longer existed and there remained no reason why any special legislation should be needed for the island.

In Newfoundland, the territorial change of 1809 still did not satisfy the fishermen of Lower Canada, and their complaints were aggravated by such measures as the Judicature Act of 1824, which empowered the Governor of Newfoundland to institute courts that administered laws with which they were unfamiliar. Eventually a compromise was reached and the British North America (Seigniorial Rights) Act was passed in 1825. It enacted that

". . . . so much of the said coast (Labrador) as lies to the westward of a line to be drawn due north and south from the bay or harbour of Ance Sablon, inclusive, as far as the fifty-second degree of north latitude, with the island of Anticosti, and all other islands adjacent to such part as last aforesaid of the coast of Labrador, shall be and the same are hereby re-annexed to and made a part of the said province of Lower Canada. . . ." (62, pp. 210-211).

Discontent and friction arising out of the effects of the Constitutional Act of 1791 were also developing in the two Canadas. By 1806 this situation was becoming strongly vocal. In Lower Canada, as might have been foreseen prior to 1791, the English-speaking residents resented being in a minority in the House of Assembly (90, p. 246). The French-speaking residents resented the immigration of English-speaking Americans into Eastern Townships (47, p. 393). The English-speaking residents feared the weakness of the disunited colonies of British North America in case of attack by a foreign power (90, p. 247). Upper Canada was dissatisfied with the distribution of revenues, for, as a result of the division of Canada in 1791, she was compelled to import all seaborne articles through territory under the administration of another government, either through Lower Canada or through the United States. Thus, trade via the St. Lawrence River was commanded by Lower Canada, and in order to collect a customs revenue, it was necessary for Upper Canada either to establish custom houses on the boundary with Lower Canada, or to come to some arrangement whereby a certain proportion of the duties levied at Quebec, which was the port of entry of Lower Canada, would be paid to the government of Upper Canada. The latter course was taken, but "numerous circumstances concur[red] to render vain any attempt permanently to regulate to the satisfaction of both Provinces the division of the Revenue" (48, p. 138). It was suggested that the boundaries of the provinces should be changed in such a way as to include Montreal in Upper Canada, thus providing it with a port of entry (90, p. 450). Some of the people of Montreal maintained that the revenue difficulties would force Upper Canada to trade increasingly with the United States, particularly in view of the canals that had been constructed in New York state, and that this might result in a movement for political union (48, p. 137).

The solution to many of these problems appeared to lie in the union of the two provinces, and in 1822 a bill was introduced into the Imperial Parliament to this effect. But there was too much opposition to it, particularly from the French-speaking inhabitants of Lower Canada, and it was withdrawn. But after petitions and counter-petitions, arguments and counter-arguments, committees, and reports, the union of the provinces was ultimately decided on. By an Act of 1840, Upper Canada and Lower Canada were reunited to form the Province of Canada.

The terms Upper and Lower Canada were still used, however, and as settlement increased and more details of the geography became known and mapped, so the need for more precision in local boundary descriptions manifested itself, as well as the necessity for considerable changes in county and township boundaries. The descriptions of such political units as lay on either side of the pre-1840 interprovincial boundary provided at the same time the detail lacking in the Order in Council that set out the boundary between Upper and Lower Canada. Thus the act "to make certain alterations in the Territorial Divisions of Upper Canada" (167) stated that the limits of the townships lying on the River Ottawa should extend to the middle of the main channel thereof, with the exception of certain islands that were specifically dealt with. Those described as "in front of" the Seigniory of La Petite Nation, and the Grand Calumet and Grand and Little Allumette Islands, for instance, remained part of Lower Canada, and the Upper Canada boundaries extended to the middle of the main channel between these islands and the south bank of the Ottawa River. Similarly, the limits of the county of Glengarry were stated as extending to the middle of Lake St. Francis and the middle of the main channel of the St. Lawrence, including the offshore islands. In the same way, a parliamentary representation act of 1853 (168) stated that the county of Huntingdon, in Lower Canada, was to be partly bounded by the River St. Lawrence "including all islands nearest to the said county and . . . opposite to the same".

At the time that these pieces of legislation were enacted, it was of course not known that Canada would be divided again; however, such boundary details as they contained were the basis of the Ontario-Quebec boundaries of today.

Disputes were still occurring between the British colonies and the United States over the interpretation of the United States boundary treaty of 1783, particularly with regard to the section of the boundary between New Brunswick and Maine. An attempt had been made to settle the matter peaceably in 1827, when it was referred to arbitration under a convention between Great Britain and the United States. The award of the arbitrator, the King of the Netherlands, was made in 1831 but was not accepted by either country. In the same year, some people attempting to hold an election under United States laws were arrested by New Brunswick authorities. In 1836 a Canadian justice of the peace was arrested by United States authorities for endeavouring to carry out his duties in what he believed to be British territory. Finally, an American official was arrested by New Brunswick authorities when he attempted to arrest British subjects who were cutting timber in the Aroostook region; this action resulted in something little short of actual war between New Brunswick and Maine—the so-called Aroostook War (193, p. 814).

In 1842, however, when Lord Ashburton, on behalf of Great Britain, paid a special visit to the United States to settle boundary problems, final agreement was reached on the remaining doubts that had sprung from the Treaty of 1783, and with the Oregon Treaty of 1846, the boundaries of British North America with the United States from the Bay of Fundy to the Gulf of Georgia were at last delimited satisfactorily, apart from minor details.

THE WEST COAST

In spite of the Oregon Treaty of 1846, the British still considered it necessary to consolidate their territory on the Pacific coast north of the 49th Parallel. In 1849, a Crown Grant of Vancouver Island was made to the Hudson's Bay Company, provided it would establish a colony thereon, and Governor Blanshard was empowered by his commission to exercise jurisdiction not only over Vancouver Island, but also all adjacent islands between the 49th and 52nd degrees of north latitude (82, p. 270).

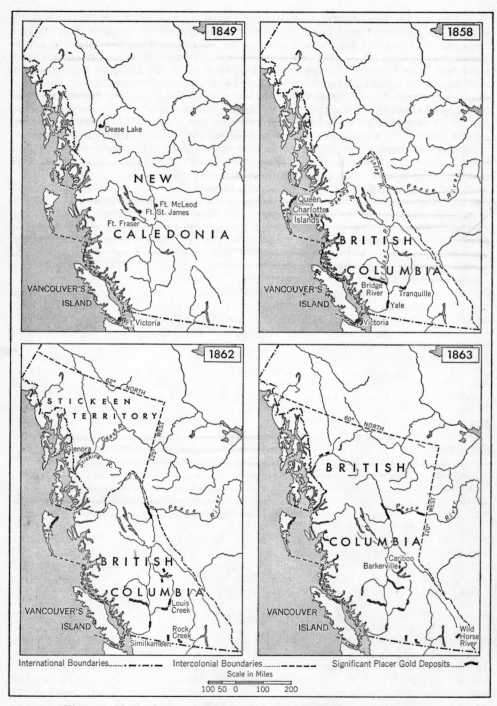

Figure 6. The evolution of the boundaries of British Columbia, 1849-1863.

The matter was accentuated by the discovery of gold in the area. As early as 1850, Governor Blanshard had reported the existence of gold on Queen Charlotte Islands, which in 1852 resulted in Governor Douglas being commissioned as Lieutenant-Governor of the island. Although this commission was not intended to sanction the colonization of the island, the act became important in 1858, when the remainder of what is now southern British Columbia became another crown colony. This step had been forced upon the British Government through the discovery of more gold on Fraser River and in the Cariboo district. This resulted in an influx of an estimated 30,000 (143, p. 302) miners into an area with a white population of about 750 only, of whom 300 were at Victoria. The Indian population was about 15,000, and one of the dangers of the gold rush was that it might produce difficulties between the natives and the whites and lead to disorder. But a far greater political danger was the fact that most of the incoming miners were Americans, and Governor Douglas was fearful they might try to establish an independent government that might become annexed to the United States. The British Government, therefore, on July 1, 1858, introduced a Bill "to provide for the government of New Caledonia". The boundaries then laid down were: on the south, the frontier of the United States; on the west the Pacific Ocean; on the north, the 55th parallel; and on the east, the watershed between the streams that flowed into the Pacific and those that flowed into the Atlantic and Arctic Oceans.

However, an amendment was proposed extending these boundaries because it was thought that the gold found on Fraser River was only a trifling indication of that to be found at its headwaters, which rose north of the 55th parallel, and the final act "to provide for the Government of British Columbia" established the boundaries as follows:

"to the South by the frontier of the United States of America, to the East by the main chain of the Rocky Mountains, to the North by Simpson's River and the Finlay branch of the Peace River, and to the West by the Pacific Ocean, and shall include Queen Charlotte's Island and all other Islands adjacent to the said territories except as hereafter excepted . . . . No part of the Colony of Vancouver's Island, as at present established, shall be comprised within British Columbia for the purposes of this Act" (82, p. 274).

The expiration of the Hudson's Bay Company's licence in 1859 left some of the territory of British North America not included in Rupert's Land or in the British Pacific colonies without a formal government, other than the direct jurisdiction of the Imperial Government under the provisions of the Indian Territories Act of 1859. In 1862, reports of further gold discoveries on Stikine River were confirmed, and eventually the British Government decided to declare the Governor of British Columbia administrator of the Territory of Stickeen, delimited by an Order in Council as follows:

". . . . the said Stickeen territories shall comprise so much of the dominions of Her Majesty as are bounded to the west and south-west by the frontier of Russian America, to the south and south-east by the boundary of British Columbia, to the east by the 125th meridian of west longitude, and to the north by the 62nd parallel of north latitude" (165, p. 190).

The only explanation for the eastern and northern limits is that they were to be extensive enough to include the whole of the Stikine basin and any future gold discoveries to the north (82, p. 277).

By this time the British Government, in striking contrast with its policy immediately after the American Revolution, was encouraging unions of smaller administrative units, and in 1863 the decision was reached to amalgamate the western mainland possessions. In any case the Select Committee of the House of Commons on the Hudson's Bay Company had recommended, as early as 1857, that means should be provided "for the ultimate extension of the colony of

Vancouver's Islands over any portion of the adjoining mainland to the west of the Rocky mountains, on which permanent settlement may be found practicable". The creation of two separate colonies, therefore, appears to have been merely an interim step in the full implementation of this recommendation. British Columbia was, therefore, now to comprise

"all such territories . . . . as are bounded to the South by the territories of the United States of America, to the West by the Pacific Ocean and the frontier of the Russian Territories in North America, to the North by the sixtieth parallel of north latitude, and to the East, from the boundary of the United States northwards, by the Rocky Mountains and the one hundred and twentieth meridian of west longitude, and shall include Queen Charlotte Island and all other Islands adjacent to the said Territories, except Vancouver Island and the Islands adjacent thereto" (135, p. 1).

No explanation was offered for the withdrawal from the 62nd to the 60th parallel as the northern boundary, but the fact that the latter parallel is the nearest convenient one to the commencement of the boundary along the 141st Meridian, established in the 1825 treaty with Russia, may have influenced this decision (82, p. 279). Moreover, gold mining on Stikine River was almost over by 1863. Access to Glenora, which had become the centre of the gold rush, was not easy, and the journey to it from Victoria took from 3 weeks to a month. Also the mining season was short, mining operations on the river being possible only between July and October. Consequently, "there were never more than 500 miners on the Stikine" (72, p. 331) and the "rush" soon subsided. Thus it may have been decided that there was no need for the northern boundary of British Columbia to extend as far north as 62 degrees north. The extension of the eastern boundary from the 125th to the 120th meridian was made so as to include the gold districts discovered in the Peace River area in 1862. The chief mining camps were on Peace River itself and on Vital, Germansen, and Manson Creeks. British Columbia and Vancouver Island were united as one colony in 1866, when the latter expressed a willingness to unite with the mainland, and hence the boundaries of British Columbia as they are known today came into being.

Thus, immediately prior to Canadian Confederation, the boundaries of British North America between the United States of America and the Russian territory of Alaska were delimited, apart from a few minor sections. British North America itself was politically divided by the boundaries of British Columbia, Canada, New Brunswick, Nova Scotia, Prince Edward Island, and Newfoundland. The remaining area was either under the control of the Hudson's Bay Company, being made up of Rupert's Land and the Northwest Territory, or directly under the British Government.

Figure 7. The extent of the territory of the Hudson's Bay Company according to a map
by J. Arrowsmith, published in 1857.

CHAPTER IV

INTERNATIONAL AND NATIONAL BOUNDARIES

The year 1867 marks the beginning of the political development of Canada as a separate State, for by the terms of the British North America Act a federal union of the Provinces of Canada, New Brunswick, and Nova Scotia came into being. These political units retained the boundaries that had already been established, with the exception that the former Province of Canada was divided into the Provinces of Ontario and Quebec, the line of division between them being identical with the line of division that had existed between Upper and Lower Canada from 1791 to 1840, following the Constitutional Act, and that had been modified during the period of their Union from 1840 to 1867.

In 1868, the Rupert's Land Act authorized the acquisition by the Dominion of Canada of "Rupert's Land and the North-Western Territory" although the full title to these territories was not transferred from the Hudson's Bay Company to Canada until 1870, and they were not actually transferred until 1871. A few days after this, British Columbia entered the federal union, and in 1873 Prince Edward Island followed. The boundaries of British Columbia remained exactly as previously defined and the boundaries of Prince Edward Island, of course, presented no difficulty.

THE NORTHERN LIMITS OF CANADA

An outstanding problem, however, was the limit of "Rupert's Land and the North-Western Territory", particularly on the north. This problem was brought into focus in 1874, when an American naval officer applied for a mining claim on the shores of Cumberland Sound, Baffin Island. As a result, the British Colonial Secretary asked the government of Canada if it wished to have the British territories adjacent to those of the Dominion on the North American continent formally annexed to Canada so as to exercise "such surveillance ... as may be necessary to prevent the occurrence of lawless acts" in the area (117, p. 10).

A second request was made, meantime, for a grant of land in Baffin Island for fishing and mining, and eventually the Canadian government informed the Colonial Office that it was "desirous of including within the boundaries of the Dominion, the territories referred to, with the islands adjacent"—a decision that was incorporated into a Canadian Order in Council dated October 9, 1874. There followed an interchange of correspondence between London and Ottawa as to the precise manner in which the transfer should take place, and a Canadian Order in Council dated April 30, 1875, suggested that an Imperial Act of Parliament should be passed defining the eastern and northern boundaries of the territory to be transferred and that the northern boundary should be "the utmost limit of the continent of America, including the islands appertaining thereto" and the eastern boundary should allow for the possible inclusion of "such portion of the North West coast of Greenland as may belong to Great Britain by right of discovery or otherwise" (117, p. 11). Matters proceeded slowly, however. The British Colonial Secretary endeavoured to accelerate them by referring to the United States mining expedition to Baffin Island, which had taken place in the meantime, without official permission, and was said to have obtained graphite and mica worth over $100,000. He further pointed out that reports had appeared in the newspapers drawing the attention of United States citizens to the northern territories and to the American expeditions that had been sent to explore certain parts of them. This American activity in the north had begun in the 1850s when the Americans joined the British in the search for Sir John Franklin (Figure 8), but some of Hall's journeys (1860-62, 1864-69, and 1871-73) had occurred after Confederation. As a result, the Colonial Secretary felt that great difficulty would be experienced in including the far northern area in Canada unless steps were speedily taken to place the title of Canada "upon a clear and unmistakable footing" (117, p. 12).

Consequently, on May 3, 1878, resolutions were carried in the Canadian Parliament to authorize the acceptance by Canada of the northern territories, although at least one member opposed the move on the grounds of expense. An address was, therefore, made to the Queen from the Senate and Commons of Canada requesting a definition of the northeasterly, northerly, and northwesterly boundaries of Canada (92, p. 9). This resulted in an Imperial Order in Council, dated July 31, 1880, which included the following statement:

"From and after September 1, 1880, all British territories and possessions in North America, not already included within the Dominion of Canada, and all islands adjacent to any of such territories or possessions, shall (with the exception of the Colony of Newfoundland and its dependencies) become and be annexed to and form part of the said Dominion of Canada . . ." (92, p. 10).

This, in effect, passed British rights to the Arctic islands to Canada, but it did not definitely describe the territory added to Canada.

Meanwhile, a notable British expedition, under Captain Sir G. S. Nares, had explored the northern coasts of Ellesmere Island and Greenland in 1875-76, and Americans had also continued their activities in the far north. Schwatka explored King William Island in 1878-80 and Greely (1881-84) explored much of Ellesmere Island (Figure 9).

In 1884, some 3½ years after the northern islands had been transferred to Canada, the Canadian government sent an expedition to the north in the D.G.S. *Neptune* under the command of Lieutenant A. R. Gordon. Its main purpose was to investigate the sea route to Churchill through Hudson Bay. Scientific stations were established in Hudson Strait, where observers spent the winter of 1884-85 (160, pp. 189-229). In 1885 (158) and 1886 (159) the work continued in the *Alert*, again under the command of Lieutenant Gordon, and many of the islands in Hudson Bay and Strait as well as settlements in what is now northern Newfoundland, Quebec, Ontario, and Manitoba were visited and reported on.

However, despite these expeditions, Canada appears to have given no documentary recognition to the fact that her boundaries had been extended until 1895, when an Order in Council constituting certain provisional districts was passed.

The boundaries of the District of Franklin were described as follows:

"Beginning at cape Best, at the entrance to Hudson strait from the Atlantic; thence westerly through said strait, Fox channel, gulf of Boothia, Franklin strait, Ross strait, Simpson strait, Victoria strait, Dease strait, Coronation gulf and Dolphin and Union strait, to a point in the Arctic sea, in longitude about 125°30′ west, and in latitude about 71° north; thence northerly including Baring Land, Prince Patrick island and the Polynea islands; thence northeasterly to the 'farthest of Commander Markham's and Lieutenant Parr's sledge journey' in 1876, in longitude about 63½° west, and latitude about 83¼° north; thence southerly through Robeson channel, Kennedy channel, Smith sound, Baffin bay and Davis strait to the place of beginning" (92, p. 12).

But the description in this Order in Council was defective, for although the districts of Yukon and Mackenzie were so delimited as to include the northern part of the continent with all the islands within 3 geographical miles, the description of Franklin was not so worded as to include all the islands more than 3 miles from the mainland. Yet the Order maintained that its effect was to divide into provisional districts all the unorganized and unnamed parts of Canada. Its actual effect, however, was virtually to declare that certain islands in the Arctic Ocean were *not* part of Canada, and an amending Order in Council dated December 18, 1897, corrected the former description of the districts of Yukon and Mackenzie so that they included the islands for 20 miles from the coast, and Franklin all the others, thus:

"all those lands and islands comprised between the one hundred and forty-first meridian of longitude west of Greenwich on the west and Davis strait, Baffin bay, Smith sound, Kennedy channel and Robeson channel on the east which are not included in any other provisional district" (92, p. 16).

By this time a fourth Canadian government expedition had sailed north, for in June 1897 the *Diana* left Halifax under Commander William Wakeham. Like the Gordon expeditions, this was concerned with the Hudson Bay route, but it sailed as far as a group of whaling stations in Cumberland Sound, eastern Baffin Island. Wakeham's farthest north was Kekerten Island (65° 42′ N.) where he "landed and hoisted the Union Jack in the presence of the agent, a number of our own officers and crew, and the Esquimaux, formally declaring in their presence that the flag was hoisted as an evidence that Baffin's Land with all the territories, islands and dependencies adjacent to it were now, as they always had been since their first discovery and occupation, under the exclusive sovereignty of Great Britain" (137, p. 24).

Thus it is from 1897, from the Canadian point of view at least, that the present land area definitely extended to the Arctic Ocean, although at this time no specific mention seems to have been made of any claim to undiscovered islands or to a formal extension of Canada to the North Pole. Any thought of claiming part of Greenland, however, appears to have been given up.

This early period in Canada's growth is interesting in that the pattern of expansion paralleled so closely that which occurred when various parts of the country had been claimed for Spain, Portugal, France, and England. The initial interest in the trade route through Hudson Strait and Bay is reminiscent of the European powers' desire to find a Northwest Passage and Wakeham's proclamation of sovereignty hardly differed from those of the 16th century explorers. Canada had quickly become a "colonial power". She had inherited more than mere territory from her motherlands—she had inherited their very motives and methods for consolidating her territorial acquisitions.

THE ALASKAN BOUNDARY

The year 1867 was important not only because confederation was then achieved. It was important also from the point of view of Canada's boundary development, because in that year the United States purchased Russia's North American territorial possessions. The landward boundaries of Alaska were those described in the convention of 1825 between Russia and Great Britain. The language of this description is clear with regard to that part of the boundary running along the 141st Meridian, but disputes arose over the interpretation of the remainder of the description. The original description was probably based on Vancouver's chart, the information on which had been greatly supplemented since 1794. In the light of this newer information, the description was defective, and the resulting disputes were accentuated when the value of the natural resources of the area was realized. One of the earliest problems resulted from the discovery of gold in the Cassiar district of British Columbia, the only practical access to which was via Stikine River, which involved passing through United States territory (*See* Figure 6). In 1872 and 1874, the Government of

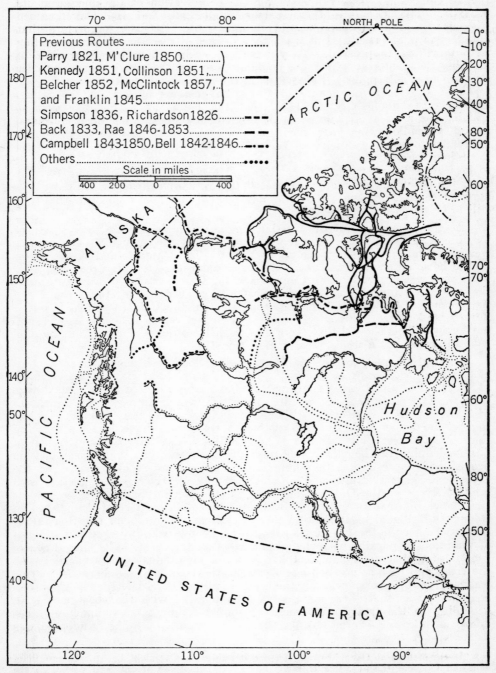

Figure 8. Major voyages of discovery and exploration in western Canada between 1814 and 1867. (The name "McClintock" is sometimes spelled "M'Clintock").

British Columbia officially pressed for the demarcation of the boundary (79, p. 190). The area was then sparsely populated, and the United States recognized that if no action was taken until more settlement occurred serious antagonism might result. But when they estimated the cost of the survey they were unwilling to proceed. They were not even willing to compromise by marking the points at which the boundary crossed the rivers falling into the Pacific Ocean (72, p. 365). Therefore, in the interests of working harmoniously together, the local American and Canadian customs officers on the Stikine decided quite unofficially, in 1875, that the boundary should be taken as crossing the river at a point some 2½ miles below Buck's, a Canadian trading post. In the following year, the American collector of customs at Sitka was instructed to consider Buck's as being in United States territory. But in the meantime Canada, tired of waiting for an official survey, had sent an engineer to locate the boundary on Stikine River. He fixed upon a line some 19 miles from the coast "at right angles thereto" (80, p. 248), which the United States agreed to accept *pro tem* without prejudice to the claims of either side that were still to be resolved.

As the importance of the Cassiar diggings diminished, the interest in the location of this part of the boundary lessened, but by the early 1880s gold mining was becoming important on the upper Yukon. The Chilkoot and White passes at the head of Lynn Canal were the principal routes to this area, and their possession was sought by both Canada and the United States in order to control the trade passing through them. Under a convention of 1892, the Chief Astronomer of Canada and the Superintendent of the U.S. Coast and Geodetic Survey made a reconnaissance survey of the coast region from Portland Canal northward. This showed that there was no distinct range of mountains parallel with the coast but a whole "sea of mountains".

In 1896 the rush to the gold fields of the Klondike began. Miners in tens of thousands were entering the gold fields, and as Canada claimed the territory at the head of the Lynn Canal, and United States revenue officers ruled that their regulations forbade the landing of British vessels anywhere on the shores of that inlet, friction ensued. Although Americans who entered the Yukon had to meet the demands of Canadian customs, these seem to have been less exacting than those of the United States (72, p. 356). Ultimately, the importance of finally defining the boundary was recognized, and in 1899 a joint commission provisionally agreed that the summits of Chilkoot and White passes, on the Dyea and Skagway trails, and a point on Chilkoot River at its junction with Klehini River, on the Dalton trail, were points upon the boundary. A convention between Great Britain and the United States in 1903 created an Alaskan Boundary Tribunal to attempt further settlement. The crucial question facing it was whether the treaty of 1825 called for a boundary drawn around the heads of the inlets or parallel with the general trend of the coast. The United States contended that it meant an unbroken chain of mountains exactly parallel with the coast and that as no such chain existed, the boundary should be 10 marine leagues from the shore, including the heads of all bays and inlets. The Canadian contention was that there were mountains parallel with the coast and that, according to the treaty, the boundary should follow their summits and cut across all inlets and fiords (80, p. 192). The boundary ultimately adopted was as follows:

"It commences at Cape Muzon. Thence it crosses in a straight line to the mouth of Portland Channel (Canal), this entrance being west of Wales Island, and passes up the channel to the north of Wales and Pearse Islands to the 56th parallel of latitude. Thence the line runs from one mountain summit to another, passing above the heads of all fiords. At the head of Lynn Canal it traverses White and Chilkoot Passes. Thence by a tortuous southwesterly course it reaches Mount Fairweather and thence follows the higher mountains around Yakutat Bay to Mount St. Elias" (49, p. 44).

The mountains chosen served the same purpose as the 10 marine league strip proposed by the United States, for they shut Canada off just as effectively from access to the sea. The American *lisière* still adds considerably to the difficulty of communication and shipment between British Columbia and the Yukon, and thus the decision of 1903 is still a sore point in certain Canadian circles.

ARCTIC BOUNDARIES

In the meantime exploration had been continued in the northern regions. Vast areas of new land had been discovered by an expedition under the command of Otto Sverdrup of Norway, which entered the Arctic archipelago in 1898 and began 4 years of exploratory journeys. They first passed through Smith Sound to Kane Basin and wintered in Rice Strait. In 1899, they turned south, entered Jones Sound, and wintered at Havnefiord, southern Ellesmere Island. Sledge journeys were carried out northward to 81°N. and westward to 98°W., a cairn being erected on the west coast of Ellesmere Island and the Norwegian flag hoisted above it. The party wintered at Goose Fiord (76°48′N.; 89°W.) and in the spring of 1901 further exploration extended to 79°30′N. and 106°W. (139, p. IV). In the course of this work, the expedition discovered, explored, and named parts of Cornwallis, Finlay, King Christian, Devon, Axel Heiberg, Ellef Ringnes, and Amund Ringnes Islands—an approximate area of 100,000 square miles, possession of which was taken in the name of the King of Norway (186, pp. 449, 450). The Norwegian claim was not withdrawn until 1930, when it was abandoned on Canada's agreeing to pay the costs of the Sverdrup expedition.

In the spring of 1903, Canada decided to send a vessel to patrol the waters of Hudson Bay and the eastern Arctic islands to aid in the establishment of permanent stations for the collection of customs, the administration of justice, and the enforcement of Canadian law (101, p. 3). It visited the western part of Hudson Bay, Baffin Island, and Lancaster Sound, raising the Canadian flag and taking formal possession of Ellesmere Island, Devon Island, and Somerset Island. In 1906-07, Captain Bernier, in command of the *Arctic*, carried out similar operations but on a much wider scale. Proceeding to Albert Harbour, north Baffin Island, he informed the whalers there that they must take out licences under Canadian whaling regulations; he landed at no less than fifteen places, on different islands, and took formal possession of them in the name of Canada, usually by raising the flag, reading a formal document, erecting a cairn, and depositing in it the document of possession. Whenever natives were encountered they were informed that they were Canadians and were expected to conform to the laws of Canada. Customs duties were collected from whalers to the extent of several hundred dollars (7).

While Bernier was still in the Arctic, Senator Pascal Poirier (possibly with the Order in Council of 1897 in mind), speaking in the Canadian Senate, on February 20, 1907, moved that the time had come for Canada to make a formal declaration of possession of the lands and islands situated in the north country, and extending to the North Pole. The senator based his proposal mainly on the fact that discovery of the Arctic islands had been made chiefly by the British whose rights Canada had inherited. But the fifteen or so expeditions to the north following Confederation had included those of the Norwegian, Sverdrup, and several Americans, and it was these more recent events that were focusing public attention on the far north.

In the course of his speech, Senator Poirier maintained that all the islands between 141 and 60 degrees west longitude up to the North Pole were Canadian territory. He suggested that the division of the Arctic area according to what

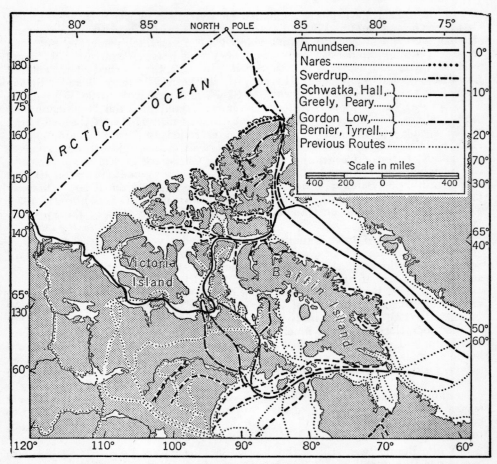

Figure 9. Major voyages of discovery and exploration in northern Canada between 1867 and 1906.

has since become known as the "sector principle" would reduce international conflict in the area; that the Arctic islands might prove a valuable asset to Canada should minerals be discovered there or the climate get warmer; and, finally, he drew attention to the fact that Canada's east and west coasts were restricted by the southward extension of Alaska and the northern extension of Newfoundland's dependency, Labrador, which was not then part of Canada, and that it might eventually become necessary "to have the North Pole as a way out of the Dominion".

This proposal has assumed great significance in modern times, not only because it applies to Canadian claims over a particular part of the earth's surface but also because it propounded the "sector principle". Although, as a result of the senator's statements, Canada is generally credited as being the first country to lay claim to a sector of either of the Polar regions, it should be noted that the so-called sector principle is merely a variation of a theme quite common in the evolution of North American boundaries.

It has already been shown that in various areas of Canada proclamations of sovereignty had been made from early times, and that the areas included in such proclamations were often defined merely by parallels of latitude or longitude or both. The Treaty of Tordesillas began with a line of longitude, the early French boundary documents with lines of latitude. The sector claim merely used two lines of longitude as the east-west limits of a proclamation of sovereignty. The southern limit was an area which was known and over which sovereignty was established; the northern limit was the Pole. Thus the "sector principle" was merely a variation of a standard method used throughout the history of Canada to extend political sovereignty from a settled area to an unknown area. To claim unknown lands was not new. Jeffreys, in 1761, for example, maintained that Canada's limits to the west extended "over countries and nations hitherto undiscovered" (123, p. 55). The Duc de la Rochefoucauld (1795) went even further, and stated that Upper Canada comprised "all the known and unknown countries extending as far as the Pacific . . . and is bounded also northwards by unknown countries" (123, p. 55). Others (123, p. 54) maintained that "as to Canada, or New France, the French would scarce admit it had any bounds to the north on this side of the pole".

Hence, not even the idea of Canada extending to the Pole was new in Poirier's speech. What made the speech so notable was the fact that it was a quasi-official public utterance, whereas previous official records of the northern limits of Canada had been by Order in Council, and the fact that it was a statement of sovereignty made in the 20th century but in the manner of the 16th century.

However, Senator Poirier's proposal was not adopted, and the Minister of the Interior dissociated himself from it (36, p. 276).

In the following year Captain Bernier again sailed north, and on Dominion Day, 1909, he and his crew "assembled around Parry's rock to witness the unveiling of a tablet placed on the rock, commemorating the annexing of the whole of the Arctic archipelago" (8, p. 192); (See Plate IV A and B). The tablet reads, in part, as follows:

"This Memorial is erected today to commemorate the taking possession for the Dominion of Canada of the whole Arctic Archipelago lying to the north of America from longitude 60 degrees west to 141 degrees west up to latitude 90 degrees north" (8, p. 195).

The Polar claims do not appear to have been officially stated in public until June 1925, when the Minister of the Interior stated, on several occasions, during debates in the House of Commons, that Canada claimed "right up to the Pole" (44a, pp. 3773, 4069, 4083). He also defined the longitudinal limits of the claim and tabled a map showing its extent. In December 1953, the Prime Minister of Canada reiterated the claim during House of Commons debate when he said:

"We must leave no doubt of our active occupation and exercise of our sovereignty in these northern lands right up to the pole" (45a, p. 700).

Lines delimiting the sector have subsequently appeared on political maps of Canada published by the Federal Government. These it is presumed, however, should merely be regarded as lines of allocation, which are delimited through the high seas or unexplored areas for the purpose of allocating lands without conveying sovereignty over the high seas.

TERRITORIAL WATERS

Senator Poirier's proposal might have raised a discussion on the whole question of territorial waters, for although his sector claim is presumed to apply only to land within the sector, the presence of the sector boundaries on official maps almost implies a claim to the "high seas" forming part of the Arctic Ocean, over which it has always been presumed that it is impossible for national sovereignty to exist.

THE FISHERIES DISPUTES

Territorial waters, as such, had been involved incidentally in disputes between Great Britain and the United States over the North Atlantic coast fishery since 1782. It has already been pointed out that following the American Revolution the inhabitants of the United States had been given equal rights with British subjects to fish in all British North American waters, except that the Americans were not permitted to dry and cure fish on the island of Newfoundland. At the conclusion of the War of 1812, the British claimed that the United States had forfeited these rights, and in 1818 a new treaty was agreed upon; this restricted the Americans to fishing on the south coast of Newfoundland from Cape Ray to the Rameau Islands; on the western and northern coast from Cape Ray to the Quirpon Islands, on the shores of the Magdalen Islands, and on the coasts, bays, harbours, and creeks from Mount Joly on the south coast of Labrador to and through the Strait of Belle Isle and thence northward indefinitely along the coast (196, p. 684). At the same time, American fishermen were given the liberty to dry and cure fish in any of the unsettled parts of these sections of the coasts of Newfoundland and Labrador. Elsewhere, the United States renounced the right of fishing or drying or curing fish on, or within 3 marine miles of, any of the coasts, bays, creeks, or harbours of British North America.

In this treaty no explanation or definition of the term "bays" was given, or any method of determining the line from which the 3 marine miles was to be measured. In interpreting the treaty, Great Britain contended that "bays" meant all those waters that, in 1818, every fisherman and mariner knew as bays, and claimed that the 3-mile limit should be measured from a line joining the headlands of such waters. The United States, on the other hand, maintained that the bays should be confined to small indentations and that the 3-mile limit should be measured from a line following the sinuosities of the coast.

In these circumstances, trouble resulted whenever the British authorities seized American vessels for alleged illegal fishing, and disputes of varying seriousness occurred. Ultimately, Great Britain and the United States agreed

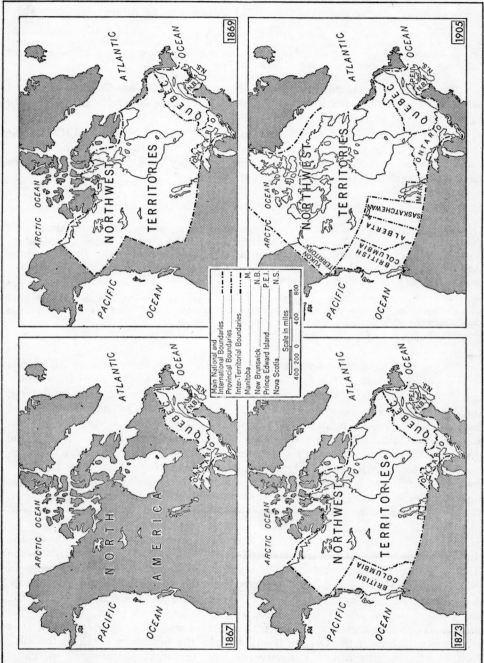

Figure 10. The major political boundaries of Canada, 1867-1905.

to submit all points in controversy to arbitration by the Hague Tribunal, for settlement in accordance with International Law. Of the seven decisions the tribunal made, that concerning territorial waters was as follows:

"In the case of bays the three marine miles are to be measured from a straight line drawn across the body of water at the place where it ceases to have the configuration and characteristics of a bay. At all other places the three marine miles are to be measured following the sinuosities of the coast" (196, p. 716).

They also recommended a series of lines drawn from headland to headland of the bays in dispute, marking out definitely the points beyond which American fishermen could not go.

In a treaty signed by Great Britain and the United States in 1912, it was agreed that so far as they were applicable to Canada, these recommendations would become effective, except that Hudson Bay and Newfoundland were specifically excluded from the agreement.

WATER BOUNDARIES WITH THE UNITED STATES

While the fisheries controversy had been going on, water boundaries with the United States had been creating difficulties. The first of these arose out of the interpretation of the language of a treaty, this time over the boundary through the Gulf of Georgia to the Pacific Ocean, which was described in the Oregon Treaty of 1846 as follows:

"to the middle of the channel which separates the continent from Vancouver's Island; and thence southerly through the middle of the said channel, and of Fuca's strait to the Pacific Ocean: Provided, however, that the navigation of the whole of the said channel and straits, south of the forty-ninth parallel of north latitude, remain free and open to both parties" (75, p. 81).

There was no single obvious "channel", owing to the existence of islands in the southern part of the Gulf of Georgia. Two, however, were in common use, Rosario Strait, between the major islands and the continental mainland, and Canal de Haro, between the islands and Vancouver Island. The first of these routes had been more frequently used in the days of sailing vessels and the British claimed that the boundary should pass through it. It was the channel marked on Vancouver's chart, and presumably, therefore, that to which the negotiators of the Oregon treaty must have referred. Canal de Haro, on the other hand, had become more popular with the increasing use of steamships, and the United States maintained that the boundary should run through it. The problem really involved the sovereignty of the islands between the mainland and Vancouver Island. The largest of these was San Juan. It was used only by Indians until 1850, apart from the fact that some cattle belonging to the Hudson's Bay Company were pastured there (2, p. 612). But in 1850 the Hudson's Bay Company established a salmon cannery on the island, and in 1851 a post. Various incidents occurred between the British and Americans, each occupying and administering the island when they could, and with the end of the United States Civil War, official action was taken to settle the matter. The main argument of the United States was that the only reason that led the negotiators of the Oregon treaty to take the boundary south of the 49th Parallel was to give all of Vancouver Island to Great Britain (89, p. 236). The problem was referred to arbitration by the Emperor of Germany, who in 1872 rendered an award in favour of the United States.

On the opposite side of the continent, there was still some doubt as to the exact course of the boundary in Passamaquoddy Bay. This was corrected by the treaty concluded between Great Britain and the United States on May 21, 1910.

"which laid down the position of the line by courses and distances, starting from a point between Treat Island and Campobello Island—and running thence in a general southerly direction to the middle of Grand Manan Channel. Popes Folly Island and the lighthouse between Woodward Point and Cranberry Point were left within United States territory" (49, p. 22).

THE LIMITS OF CANADIAN TERRITORIAL WATERS

Territorial waters again became a significant factor in October 1932, when the activities of the Royal Canadian Mounted Police in dealing with smugglers made it necessary to consider the question of the extent of Canadian territorial waters. Using generally accepted terminology[1], territorial waters are the marginal seas within 3 marine miles of the coast of Canada or of base lines delimiting the national waters of Canada, as determined in accordance with international law and practice. National waters mean the waters that form part of the national territory of Canada. It will be recalled that, in 1910, the Hague Tribunal had made certain decisions and awards regarding the boundaries between national and territorial waters, where they were adjacent, in so far as they concerned the North Atlantic Fishing Limits under the Treaty of 1818 between Great Britain and the United States. The problem that faced the Canadian government in 1932 was that such boundaries needed to be defined for the areas not considered by the Hague Tribunal. In 1937, an Order in Council was passed that set forth the unanimous views and recommendations of a Committee of the Privy Council in relation to the delimitation of territorial waters in respect of the St. Lawrence estuary and of the bays, gulfs, and straits of Nova Scotia, New Brunswick, and Prince Edward Island, the Pacific coast, and Hudson Bay and Strait. It is noteworthy that in the case of the bays, gulfs, and straits in Nova Scotia, New Brunswick, and Prince Edward Island, the base lines were drawn in accordance with the recommendations of the Hague Tribunal. It is also to be noted that in the St. Lawrence estuary the base line from which territorial waters were to be measured was "a line drawn from Cape Rosieres on the Gaspe Peninsula to the west end of the Island of Anticosti to the mouth of the River St. John". Hudson Bay and Strait were regarded as national waters, as territorial waters were to be measured from a line "from Button Island to Hatton Headland on Resolution Island". This was presumably on the grounds that Hudson Bay and Strait together constitute an "historic bay", as although the entrance to them is about 32 miles wide, historically sovereignty was asserted over the area by Great Britain and France and was implied by the Hudson's Bay Company's charter. Furthermore, Hudson Bay and Strait had been specifically included in the districts of Ungava, Keewatin, and Franklin as defined by the Order in Council of 1897, were declared to be territorial waters of Canada by Act of Parliament in 1906 (174), and are, at the present time, an integral part of the Northwest Territories.

---

[1] The terminology used recently in "An Act to Protect the Coastal Fisheries" differs slightly from this. In this Act "Canadian territorial waters" means any water designated by any Act of the Parliament of Canada or by the Governor-in-Council as the territorial waters of Canada, or any waters not so designated being within 3 marine miles of any of the coasts, bays, creeks, or harbours of Canada, and includes the inland waters of Canada (182).

Finally, it will be noted that no action was then to be taken with regard to Arctic waters. Senator Poirier's "sector", therefore, still remains in an indefinite official state, but it has recently come to take on added meaning with the possibility that large areas of sea ice may be used as airfields. If this becomes a reality, then the question of sovereignty over the ice in "Poirier's sector" will no doubt have to be examined, for it will have some of the aspects and uses of dry land.

INTERNATIONAL ADJUSTMENTS

Article V of the 1908 Treaty concerning the boundary between the United States and Canada provided for the survey and demarcation of the boundary. The survey showed the necessity for certain minor adjustments. These were made the basis of a further treaty, which was signed at Washington on February 24, 1925.

The first of these adjustments concerned Lake of the Woods. Surveys showed that the line drawn south from the northwestern point of the lake intersected the water boundary in Northwest Angle Inlet in five places "adjacent to and directly south of the said northwesternmost point, and that there are two small areas of United States waters in Lake of the Woods, comprising a total area of two and one-half acres, entirely surrounded by Canadian waters" (77, p. 11). No permanent monuments were ever erected on the boundary lines north of the most southerly of these points of intersection, so that the southernmost of them was adopted in lieu of the previously established northwesternmost point. By this change Canada gained the 2½ acres of water area.

The second adjustment concerned the lines between monuments established on the 49th Parallel east of the Rocky Mountains. They had been established as curved lines, following the parallel, in 1908 but were now changed to straight lines. By this change Canada lost about 30 acres of land.

The third adjustment was made to extend the boundary in Passamaquoddy Bay seaward to the limit of territorial waters of Canada and the United States. By this, Canada gained a water area of about 9 acres.

THE LABRADOR BOUNDARY

If one were to accept the "sector principle" as having settled Canada's northern boundaries, the only major outstanding boundary problem by 1927 concerned Labrador, a "dependency" of the island of Newfoundland. The original acquisition of this dependency dates from the Royal Proclamation of 1763, but it was transferred to Quebec in 1774 and back to Newfoundland in 1809, and changes were made in its extent in 1825. Thus Labrador was "tossed back and forth like a shuttlecock" (105, p. 160) but in these see-sawings it is significant that each time control was returned to Newfoundland the territory it regained was reduced by an area predominantly occupied by French Canadians, who undoubtedly objected to English law. That any territory ever passed back to Newfoundland was probably due to a similar dislike on the part of Newfoundland fishermen for Quebec law. By the Labrador Act of 1809, Newfoundland lost the Magdalen Islands, and by the Labrador Act of 1825, Anticosti and part of the north shore of the St. Lawrence, but a certain part of Labrador was repeatedly re-annexed to Newfoundland. Apart from the modification of 1825, this part must have had the same extent as it had in 1763. Whatever its area, it must have been sufficiently great for the administration of justice, so far as it affected the fishermen (193, p. 916).

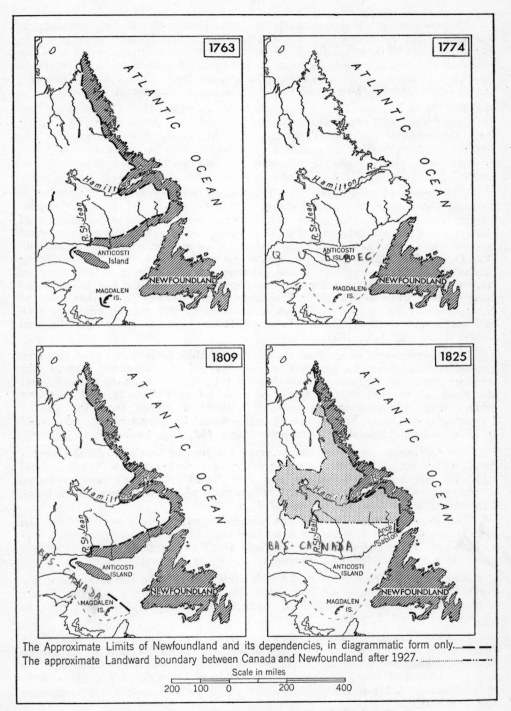

The Approximate Limits of Newfoundland and its dependencies, in diagrammatic form only.
The approximate Landward boundary between Canada and Newfoundland after 1927.

Scale in miles

200   100   0   200   400

Figure 11. The evolution of the boundaries of Newfoundland.

However, no attempt was made to define clearly the inland boundary of Labrador. The issue was first raised in 1888 by Robert Pinsent, a judge of the Supreme Court of Newfoundland, when he observed a discrepancy between the extent of Newfoundland's jurisdiction in Labrador as defined by the Newfoundland Letters Patent of 28th March, 1876, and as shown by a map of Labrador published in 1880 by the authority of the Canadian Minister of the Interior.

The 1876 Letters Patent appointed Sir Stephen Hill Governor of the "Island of Newfoundland, and the islands adjacent, and all the coast of Labrador from the entrance of Hudson's Straits to a line to be drawn due north and south from Ance Sablon on the said coast to the fifty-second degree of north latitude, and all the islands adjacent to that part of the said coast of Labrador. . . ." (62, II, p. 754).

This appeared to Pinsent to allot a much smaller area of Labrador to Newfoundland than the map indicated, and he considered that the matter should be rectified so that there would be no doubt as to the jurisdiction of the courts of Newfoundland. The Department of the Interior reported that the line was marked as a dotted line and described as "supposed" or "undefined" (62, II, pp. 347-349). There the matter rested, in effect, until the beginning of the twentieth century, when the existence in the interior of Labrador of timber that could be used for making paper was realized. For in 1902 the Grand River Pulp and Lumber Company obtained from the Government of Newfoundland leases to cut timber on an area of 297 square miles on both the north and south sides of Hamilton River between Lake Melville and Grand Falls (62, I, p. 132).

The Government of Quebec, on hearing of this, maintained that the area concerned was under its jurisdiction, and warned the company that all the territory south of Hamilton River belonged to the province of Quebec, that the right to cut timber there could be acquired only from it, and that any cutting upon the territory in question without a licence from the Quebec Department of Lands, Mines, and Fisheries would be considered a violation of the law and would be dealt with accordingly (62, I, p. 146).

The Quebec government also referred the matter to the Federal Government, which maintained that nothing could be included within Newfoundland Labrador but coasts and islands, and that "coast" could not possibly be so interpreted as to include the territory through which Hamilton River flows, hundreds of miles from the ocean (62, I, p. 129).

The Newfoundland government disagreed with this interpretation, but proceedings were nevertheless taken against some of the alleged "poachers" (44) and ultimately the Governments of Canada and Newfoundland agreed to submit the matter to the Judicial Committee of the Privy Council.

Newfoundland contended that the boundary should be the line drawn due north from Ance Sablon[1] as far as the 52nd degree of north latitude, thence northwards along the watershed of rivers flowing into the Atlantic Ocean, to Cape Chidley (62, I, p. 60).

Canada submitted that the boundary was a line delimiting the area of the coast accessible and useful to the fisheries and proposed that it should be located and defined as a line to be drawn from the eastern headland of the bay or harbour of Blanc Sablon, on the south, to Cape Chidley on the north, at a distance of 1 mile from high-water mark on the sea-coast of Labrador (62, I, p. 60).

---

[1] Now known as Blanc Sablon.

Both sides based their cases on the interpretation of various Orders in Council, proclamations, and statutes, but the Judicial Committee supported the "height of land" argument on several grounds (62, XII, pp. 1015-17). First of all, under international law, occupation of a sea-coast was said to carry with it a right to the whole territory drained by the rivers that empty their waters into it. Furthermore, in the absence of any specified boundary or of any special feature (such as a political frontier) that could be taken as a boundary, they recognized the difficulty of suggesting any point between the seashore and the watershed at which a line could be drawn. However, the line of the watershed running from Cape Chidley southward was for a considerable distance the eastern boundary of the Hudson's Bay Company's former territory, and so the watershed might for that distance form a "political" as well as a "natural" boundary for the "coast" of Labrador. Thirdly, in their opinion, the language of the Imperial Act of 1825 implied that the expression "coasts of Labrador" as used in 1763 and 1809 was understood by Parliament in 1825 to have comprised the country back to the watershed.

The Committee considered the Canadian contention that the boundary should be drawn 1 mile from high-water mark was unsound. A large part of this mile-wide strip lay at the summit of high cliffs, was inaccessible from the sea, and was, therefore, useless to the fishery, which, according to Canada's argument, had been the reason for allotting the coast of Labrador to Newfoundland. Secondly, access to wood for repairs was essential for the proper conduct of the fishery, and sufficient wood could be obtained for this purpose only if the fishermen were free to cut timber for an average distance of 3 miles and a maximum of 5 miles from high-water mark. This was confirmed by the practice invariably followed by the Newfoundland Government, which, when granting timber concessions on the island of Newfoundland itself, always reserved a margin of at least 3, and sometimes 5, miles for the use of fishermen. Third, the 1-mile limit was impractical because

"there are places where a broad peninsula is joined to the mainland by a neck of not more than two miles in width, and in each of these instances the one-mile strip would meet in the neck of the peninsula and cut off by an interposed barrier of Newfoundland soil all access to the Canadian enclave on the broader part of the promontory" (62, XII, p. 1018).

However, the Privy Council did not feel that the boundary claimed by Newfoundland in the south was warranted by the terms of the statute of 1825. For these and other reasons, their Lordships were of the opinion that

"the boundary between Canada and Newfoundland in the Labrador Peninsula is a line drawn due north from the eastern boundary of the bay or harbour of Ance Sablon as far as the fifty-second degree of north latitude, and from thence westward along that parallel until it reaches the Romaine River, and then northward along the left or east bank of that river and its head waters to their source and from thence due north to the crest of the watershed or height of land there, and from thence westward and northward along the crest of the watershed of the rivers flowing into the Atlantic Ocean until it reaches Cape Chidley" (62, XII, p. 1026).

As a result, Woody Island, a small island lying opposite Ance Sablon, and claimed by both Canada and Newfoundland, was awarded to Canada because it lies just west of the boundary line.

Thus, in 1927, Newfoundland's sovereignty was confirmed over an area of some 112,000 square miles of territory, and the eastern boundary of Canada was defined.

FROM SEA TO SEA

Not for long, however, was Canada to have a land boundary on the east, for in 1949 Newfoundland joined Confederation and became Canada's tenth province.

The boundaries of the new province remained essentially as they had been when Newfoundland was a separated political entity. Some changes in terminology resulted, however, for whereas it had been common to refer to the island of Newfoundland simply as "Newfoundland" and for the "Coast of Labrador" to be regarded as its dependency, both areas now had the same status, for together they formed one province. Furthermore, any Newfoundland "territorial waters" passed to the control of the Government of Canada. Exactly what these territorial waters were may be a matter of doubt. It has been mentioned earlier that the agreement between Great Britain and the United States in 1912 did not cover Newfoundland waters, but they were covered by the recommendations of the Hague tribunal and it appears unlikely that these could be successfully challenged (64, pp. 344-52).

But the entry of Newfoundland into Confederation also raised other problems with regard to Canada's territorial waters, which, in the east, had last been defined by the Order in Council of 1937. For example, should the Gulf of St. Lawrence now be declared a "mare clausum", as had been done with Hudson Bay in 1937? This question must remain pending, for the Department of External Affairs, in conjunction with other government agencies, is at present reviewing Canada's position on territorial waters as a result of recent developments. Canada has subscribed to the view that her territorial waters include the marginal sea within 3 marine miles of the base lines on the coast. But the configuration of Canada's coast is such that if this is strictly adhered to there is an international passage through such water bodies as Hudson Strait and Hudson Bay, the channels between many of the Arctic islands, and between Vancouver Island and the Queen Charlotte Islands and the mainland.

But if the entry of Newfoundland created problems with regard to territorial waters, it also refocused attention on its boundary with Quebec, which in 1949 ceased to be an international boundary and became an interprovincial one. The maps published by the province of Quebec still do not show this boundary "pour cause". Attention will, therefore, now be turned to an examination of the ways in which the other interprovincial boundaries of Canada evolved.

CHAPTER V

SETTLING THE OLDER PROVINCIAL BOUNDARIES

The boundary situations existing in Canada in 1873 are summarized in Table I. The limits of Prince Edward Island were known exactly; it had, of course, no interprovincial boundaries. The boundary between New Brunswick and Nova Scotia had been delimited and demarcated since 1858. The boundaries of British Columbia and Manitoba, and the New Brunswick-Quebec boundary, were precisely delimited, as was the boundary between Quebec and Ontario. But the western and northern boundaries of Ontario and the northern and eastern boundaries of Quebec were only loosely defined, and it was this fact that led to the first problems Canada had to face with regard to her major internal boundaries. Although the interprovincial boundaries between Nova Scotia, New Brunswick, and Quebec were settled by 1873, their settlement had been by no means a simple matter, and an examination of the problems involved in these earlier interprovincial disputes will provide a background for the remaining problems connected with Ontario and Quebec with which Canada was confronted virtually at the time of its creation.

THE NOVA SCOTIA-NEW BRUNSWICK BOUNDARY

The present boundary between New Brunswick and Nova Scotia was established in 1858-59, but there had been a division between these two parts of historic Acadia long before that. Such a division was first contemplated by Sir William Alexander in 1624, "the country of New Scotland, being dividit into twa Provinces" (126, p. 88). Alexander's own map shows Alexandria, the present New Brunswick, and Caledonia, the present Nova Scotia.

TABLE I

Boundary Situation, 1873

Boundary	Status		
	Demarcated	Precisely delimited	Generally delimited
International—			
Canada-United States	X		
Canada-United States (Alaska)			X
Canada-Newfoundland			X
Intranational—			
Quebec-New Brunswick	X		
New Brunswick-Nova Scotia	X		
Prince Edward Island	X		
Ontario-Quebec		X	
Manitoba-Ontario		X	
British Columbia-Territories		X	
Manitoba-Territories		X	
Quebec-Territories			X
Ontario-Territories			X

Figure 12. Sir William Alexander's map of New Scotland.

During the period of French occupation, between 1632 and 1636, two grants were made in Acadia. In 1632, the Company of New France granted the Bay of Fundy and the River St. Croix to De Razilly, and in 1635 they granted the territory at the mouth of St. John River to Charles La Tour. After the death of De Razilly in 1636, his rights in Acadia devolved upon his brother, who sold them to Charnisay, one of De Razilly's lieutenants. Charnisay immediately insisted upon these rights, which led to disputes with La Tour, as the boundaries of their grants overlapped. The matter was referred to the King of France, who in 1638, established boundaries between his two lieutenants in a letter to Charnisay as follows:

". . . . vous soyez mon Lieutenant général en la côte des Etchemins, à prendre depuis le milieu de la terre ferme de la Baie Françoise[1], en tirant vers les Virgines, et Gouverneur de Pentagoet; et que le charge du sieur de La Tour mon Lieutenant général en la côte d'Acadie, soit depuis le milieu de la Baie Françoise jusqu'au détroit de Canseau. . . ." (52, p. 176).

These boundaries, although still not stated with absolute precision, in effect awarded the peninsula to La Tour and the mainland to Charnisay.

Such a division was also tacitly recognized as existing between the territories of the English and French during the time when the limits of Acadia were under discussion prior to 1735, but its final adoption in 1784 was probably not influenced by the earlier use (52, p. 262).

The causes leading up to the decision to constitute New Brunswick a separate province have been fully discussed in Chapter III. When the decision was taken, in 1784, three dividing lines were considered. The line finally adopted was described in the commission dated August 16, 1784, to Thomas Carleton as Captain-General and Governor-in-Chief of New Brunswick as

". . . . to the south by a line in the centre of the Bay of Fundy, from the River St. Croix aforesaid to the mouth of the Musquat River, by the said river to its source and from thence by a due east line across the Isthmus into the Bay Verte. . . ." (61, p. 23).

This boundary appears to have been entirely satisfactory to New Brunswick, but it did not suit the authorities at Halifax at all. The boundary area, notably between Sackville and Amherst, had been settled between 1761 and 1765 by New Englanders, with later additions from Yorkshire, England. Large numbers of immigrants from the United States settled in other parts of what is now Nova Scotia at about the same time, while few went elsewhere in the New Brunswick part. Conversely, of the Loyalists who migrated to British North America in 1783, only a few went to the head of Chignecto Bay, the majority going to the St. John Valley. In Nova Scotia, where fewer Loyalists settled, the New Englanders had a proportionally greater share in the government and it was natural that these people should be regarded by Nova Scotia as "belonging" to them rather than to New Brunswick (52, pp. 367-68). The new boundary divided these "old" settlements between the two provinces, and Nova Scotia made most determined efforts to have it changed. The arguments put forward by the House of Assembly of Nova Scotia in 1792 stated that the division line was vague and indeterminate because of the many sources of Musquat River and that it inconvenienced the inhabitants of the counties of Cumberland and Westmorland by dividing their land so that some parts were subject to the government of New Brunswick and other parts to Nova Scotia. The limits of the jurisdiction of the courts in the border counties were also alleged to be difficult to determine and hence a further inconvenience. As a result, Nova Scotia was deprived of part of its revenue. No assessments could be levied and collected and the laws could be easily evaded (52, p. 365).

[1] The present Bay of Fundy.

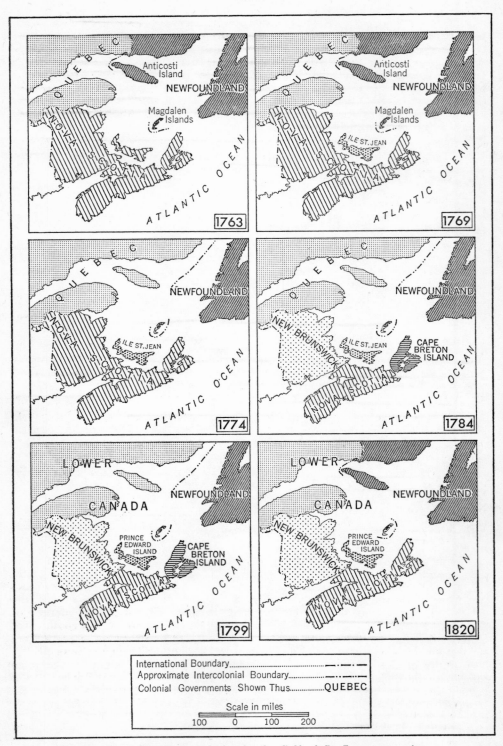

Figure 13. Boundary evolution in the Gulf of St. Lawrence region.

These arguments aroused spirited rejoinders in New Brunswick. The legislature of that province not only maintained that there had been no complaints from the inhabitants concerning the boundary, but also that it was the most natural boundary that could be drawn between the two provinces. Its whole length was less than 17 miles and the part where any possible uncertainty could exist did not exceed one-fifth of the total distance and, moreover, passed through wilderness land (52, p. 365). The controversy dragged on for several years, but no major changes were made in the boundary of 1784 and so the matter appears to have ended.

The definition of the boundary as ultimately accepted by Nova Scotia and New Brunswick and confirmed by the legislatures of both provinces, following enactment by the Imperial Government, was as follows:

"Commencing at the mouth of the Missiguash River in Cumberland Bay, and thence following the several courses of the said river to a post near Black Island, thence north fifty-four degrees twenty-five minutes East, crossing the South end of Black Island two hundred and eighty-eight chains to the South angle of Trenholm Island, thence North thirty-seven degrees East eighty-five chains and eighty-two links to a post, thence North seventy-six degrees East, forty-six chains and twenty links to the portage, thence South sixty-five degrees forty-five minutes East, three hundred and ninety-four chains and forty links to Tidnish Bridge, thence following the several courses of said river along its northern upland bank to its mouth, thence following the northwesterly channel to the deep water of the Bay Verte, giving to Nova Scotia the control of the navigable waters on Tidnish River" (52, p. 369).

This does not precisely follow the boundary described in Carleton's commission. The minor changes were probably made so as to effect a compromise that would benefit both provinces. In the upper reaches of the Missiguash the boundary runs in such a way as to give the entire river to Nova Scotia. It does not start from the source of the river, but some 2 miles to the southwest of it, thus leaving the entire highway from Cumberland Basin to Baie Verte, and the grants along it, to New Brunswick.

Probably in compensation for the allotment of this territory to New Brunswick, the line does not continue to the sea but stops at Tidnish River, which went to Nova Scotia (52, pp. 370-71).

THE NEW BRUNSWICK-QUEBEC BOUNDARY

In 1784, the northern boundary of Nova Scotia became the northern boundary of New Brunswick. As already stated, this had been defined, in 1763, as the watershed between the rivers that drained into the St. Lawrence and those that drained into the sea. In 1784, the commission to Thomas Carleton, as first Governor of New Brunswick, described the northern and western boundaries of the new province as follows:

". . . .bounded on the westward by the mouth of the River St. Croix, by the said river to its source, and by a line drawn due north from thence to the southern boundary of our Province of Quebec, to the northward, by the said boundary as far as the western extremity of the Bay des Chaleurs" (61, p. 23).

Shortly after this a controversy broke out between the surveyors-general of Quebec and New Brunswick, mainly because the seigniory of Madawaska and part of Temiscouata were south of the watershed and, therefore, according to Carleton's commission, should have gone to New Brunswick. But Quebec had been exercising some jurisdiction over these areas for many years. It was under its authority that the seigniory of Madawaska had been granted in 1683; in 1763 Quebec had issued a proclamation prohibiting all Canadians from interfering with the Indian hunting grounds above the Great Falls of the River St. John, and in 1784 an Indian had been tried by the Quebec authorities for a murder committed at Madawaska.

But at this time the boundary between British and American territory was in dispute, and it was quite apparent to the authorities that if the northern watershed were fixed as the boundary between New Brunswick and Quebec then it would have to be accepted as the boundary between Canada and the United States in the area immediately west. In these circumstances, neither New Brunswick nor Quebec would gain Temiscouata and Madawaska: these areas would go to the United States. Quite apart from the loss of this territory *per se*, it would also have meant that the invaluable line of communication through it, connecting the Maritime Provinces with the other British colonies, would be lost. In those days, when the rivers were the principal highways, St. John and Madawaska Rivers afforded the only practical link between Quebec and Halifax. In summer it was shorter, safer, and cheaper than the sea route via the St. Lawrence, and in winter it was the only practical route.

An attempt at settlement occurred in 1787, but was fruitless, and New Brunswick assumed jurisdiction over the Madawaska district and granted licences of occupation to a number of Acadians. Shortly after this, however, Governor Carleton of New Brunswick suggested that the boundary might be described so as to run from the western extremity of the Baie de Chaleur, along the River Restigouche to its source, and thence by a straight line westward to the already established watershed boundary (52, p. 380).

This suggestion of Carleton's with regard to the Restigouche was followed up by occupation, whether intentional or not. Quebec exercised jurisdiction north of its mouth and New Brunswick south of it, and as a result the river became recognized as the boundary by the people living in the area. But it was certainly never officially recognized, and the signing of the Ashburton Treaty with the United States in 1842 revived the problem, because that treaty effected a compromise with respect to the international boundary, and territory south of the highlands or watershed divide and west of the "due north line" remained in British hands. The main activities in this area were concerned with lumbering, in which not only individual citizens were interested, but also the provincial governments, as these derived a large part of their revenues from stumpage on timber cut on public lands. Some settlement had, by this time, occurred in the area, mainly under the authority of New Brunswick, whose laws were, therefore, more familiar to the new inhabitants than those of Quebec. Furthermore, the rivers were still the main means of transportation, and the southward flowing St. John and its tributaries the Madawaska and St. Francis formed the outlets for the timber and other products of the country. During the struggle with the United States over the International Boundary, New Brunswick had stoutly maintained jurisdiction over much of the area and had frustrated attempts at occupation from the state of Maine. Lower Canada (Quebec) on the other hand took no active part in these operations (60, p. 93).

But the two provinces could not agree on the disposition of the territory, so the British government appointed a commission to examine the situation. The commission, in 1848, recommended a division of the territory in dispute by prolonging the straight line of the treaty of 1842 to 47°50' N[1]., and continuing the boundary east along this parallel to Kedgewick River, which would then form the boundary with the Restigouche to the Baie de Chaleur. Part of Restigouche River was retained as the boundary because settlement had taken place in both provinces from some distance on each side of the river. The remaining part of the boundary placed most of the country in dispute in New Brunswick, to which province the commission considered it would be "beneficially and properly assigned" (60, p. 93).

---

[1] It will be noted from their map (Figure 14) that this parallel was actually north of 47°50'N.

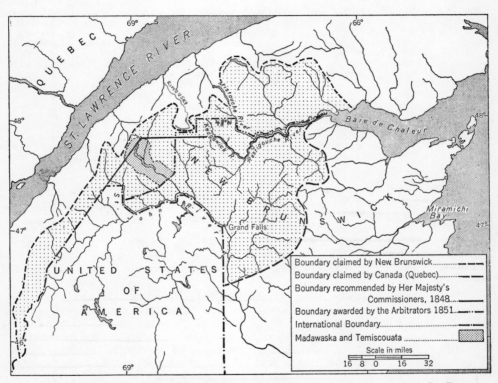

Figure 14. The Quebec-New Brunswick boundary (after a map accompanying the Report of Her Majesty's Boundary Commissioners, 1848).

But although New Brunswick was prepared to agree to the recommendations of the report, the Province of Canada was not. The British government, therefore, in 1850, suggested that two arbitrators be appointed, one by each province, to decide the question, and in 1851 they rendered their decision, which became the foundation of the boundary as it exists today. In their final judgment the arbitrators made adjustments to the satisfaction of both sides and the disputed boundary was finally settled by Imperial Act of Parliament in 1851, as follows:

"That New Brunswick shall be bounded on the West by the Boundary of the United States, as traced by the Commissioners of Boundary under the Treaty of Washington dated August 1842, from the Source of the Saint Croix to a Point near the Outlet of Lake Pech-la-wee-kaa-co-nies or Lake Beau, marked A. in the accompanying Copy of a Part of Plan 17 of the Survey of the Boundary under the above Treaty; thence by a straight Line connecting that Point with another Point to be determined at the Distance of One Mile due South from the Southernmost Point of Long Lake; thence by a straight Line drawn to the Southernmost Point of the Fiefs Madawaska and Temiscouata, and along the South-eastern Boundary of those Fiefs to the South-east Angle of the same; thence by a meridional Line Northwards till it meets a Line running East and West, and tangent to the Height of Land dividing the Waters flowing into the River Rimouski from those tributary to the Saint John; thence along this tangent Line Eastward until it meets another meridional Line tangent to the Height of Land dividing Waters flowing into the River Rimouski from those flowing into the Restigouche River; thence along this meridional Line to the 48th Parallel of Latitude; thence along that Parallel to the Mistouche River; and thence down the Centre of the Stream of that River to the Restigouche; thence down the Centre of the Stream of the Restigouche to its mouth in the Bay of Chaleurs; and thence through the Middle of that Bay to the Gulfs of the Saint Lawrence; the Islands in the said Rivers Mistouche and Restigouche to the Mouth of the latter River at Dalhousie being given to New Brunswick" (184).

By this Act, Temiscouata and the Seigniory of Madawaska were assigned to Canada, and the upper reaches of St. John River went to New Brunswick. As the southern boundary of the Seigniory was taken as the interprovincial boundary, it was deemed reasonable to extend this line westward to the International Boundary, and to award to Canada the territory lying west of the Seigniory and north of this line. The area involved was of little use to New Brunswick, and would have presented very awkward administrative problems if left under her jurisdiction.

The next part of the boundary was the northern watershed always claimed by New Brunswick, although it does not follow the natural windings of the watershed, but lines that were thought at the time to be tangential to its windings and would, therefore, be easy to demarcate. The next part of the line is the parallel of 48 degrees. This may have been chosen not only because it was an even parallel but because it was also thought to form almost another tangent line to the highlands and, as a substitute for the 47°50′ N. of the commission of 1848, it also gave some additional territory to New Brunswick in compensation for the loss of part of the Madawaska area. Also as compensation to New Brunswick, the Mistouche (later identified as the Patapedia) was chosen as part of the river boundary, as it was the first large river east of the Kedgewick, which formed part of the boundary claimed by Canada (52, p. 407).

THE LIMITS OF ONTARIO

The development of the boundary between Quebec and Ontario has already been described. It was fundamentally the same as that established when the Province of Canada was divided into Upper and Lower Canada in 1791; at the same time Upper Canada had been defined as including "the utmost extent of the country commonly called or known by the name of Canada". A proclamation by Governor Simcoe in 1792 divided Upper Canada into electoral districts and defined Kent, the westernmost one, in similar phrase-ology. As a result, when the province of Ontario was created it claimed to extend to the Rocky Mountains on the west and the Arctic slope on the north and northwest.

But after the surrender to Canada in 1870 of all territorial rights and claims of the Hudson's Bay Company, the Government of Ontario became interested in securing a more precise definition of its boundaries on the west and north. On November 3, 1869, the Lieutenant-Governor of Ontario, in his opening address to the Legislature, referred to the transfer to Canada of the Northwest Territory and suggested an early definition of the boundary line between that territory and his province (125, p. 185).

This boundary depended upon the definition of the southern limit of the Hudson's Bay Company's former territories. None of the boundaries of "Rupert's Land" and the "North-Western Territory" had ever been authoritatively determined with precision. According to the Hudson's Bay Company, Rupert's Land extended to the watershed of all rivers flowing into Hudson Bay and was so depicted on the maps drawn by Arrowsmith, the company's geographer. This appears to be the greatest extent of Rupert's Land under any reasonable interpretation.

On the other hand, in 1700, after the Treaty of Ryswick, the Hudson's Bay Company had informed the Lords of Trade and Plantations that, if it became necessary, it was willing to accept 53 degrees north, or Albany River, as its southern boundary on the west coast of the bay. The company specifically stressed, however, that "the whole streights and Bay" belonged to it by right (123, p. 123) and, as events turned out, the suggested boundary never became operative. The Government of Ontario, however, claimed this as the province's northern boundary. It maintained that the territory south of this line and north of the watershed of the Great Lakes, which was conceded by the treaties of Utrecht and Paris, reverted to the British Crown and not to the Hudson's Bay Company. The Hudson's Bay Company's employees who operated in this area after 1700 did so, Ontario maintained, as British subjects with merely the same rights and privileges as other traders (193, p. 902).

The Government of Canada, however, took the view that the height of land between the St. Lawrence and Hudson Bay constituted the northern boundary of Ontario. This skirted the northern shores of Lakes Superior and Nipigon at distances of from 15 to 50 miles.

The western boundary depended upon the interpretation of various Acts of Parliament, Royal Proclamations, and Commissions since 1763. Ontario con-tended that the boundary was a due north line from the source of the Mississippi (approximately 95°14' W.). This contention was based on Sir Guy Carleton's Commission as Governor of Quebec, issued a few months after the Quebec Act of 1774, which described his government as extending from the confluence of the Ohio and Mississippi northward along the eastern bank of the Mississippi to the southern boundary of the Hudson's Bay Company's territories. But the Federal Government defined this eastern boundary as the prolongation of a due north line from the confluence of the Ohio and the Mississippi. This inter-pretation was based on the phrase in the Quebec Act of 1774 that defined the boundary of Quebec as extending along the bank of the Ohio River "Westward, to the Banks of the Mississippi, and Northward to the Southern Boundary of the Territory granted to the Merchants Adventurers of England, trading to Hudson's Bay" (161, p. 571). By this interpretation the boundary would be in approximate longitude 89°9' W. The country between this meridian and that claimed by Ontario, about 275 miles in width from east to west, became known as "The Disputed Territory".

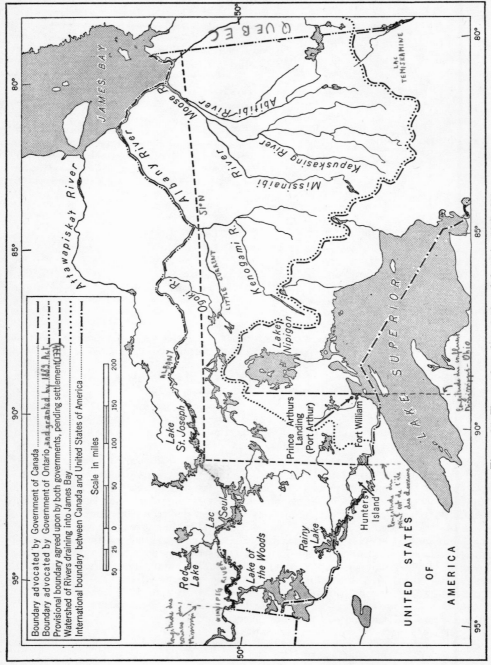

Figure 15. The northern boundaries of Ontario, 1867-1889.

The Federal boundary would have divided the existing settlements on the shores of Thunder Bay and alienated from Ontario a large area over which it had for some time been exercising jurisdiction. Even by 1857, over 25,000 acres of land had been patented by the Province of Canada on the north shore of Lake Superior west of longitude 88°50' W. By the time of Confederation an additional 10,000 acres had been patented in the same area, and included the village of Prince Arthur's Landing, the settlement around Fort William (the site of the projected terminus of the Canadian Pacific Railway), and the townships of Blake, Crooks, Pardee, Paiponge, Oliver, Neeling, and McIntyre. If the "Disputed Territory" were not awarded to Ontario, all of this rapidly developing area would be excluded from that province, leaving to it a narrow strip north of the Great Lakes and south of the height of land (122, p. 2).

In 1872 the Government of Ontario was called upon by the Federal Department of Public Works to pay for the maintenance of a police force at Thunder Bay and for construction at Prince Arthur's Landing. The payments were made, but, because the areas to which they referred were being claimed by the Federal Government, Ontario asked under what authority the expenditures in question had been made (123, p. 346).

This led to provisional boundaries being agreed on; these were confirmed by Orders in Council of both governments, in 1874, as follows:

"On the West:—the meridian line passing through the most easterly point of Hunter's Island, run south until it meets the Boundary Line between the United States and Canada, and north until it intersects the fifty-first parallel of latitude; and the said fifty-first parallel of latitude shall be the Conventional Boundary of the Province of Ontario on the North" (123, p. 347).

The westerly provisional line thus agreed upon was at about 91 degrees west longitude.

In 1878, in an endeavour to settle the question, three arbitrators were chosen and their conclusions became known as "The Award". The terms, which were satisfactory to the province of Ontario, were accepted by that province on March 11, 1879, by 42 Vict. Cap. 2, but the legislation necessary to give them binding effect was not passed by the Federal Government and the Award, therefore, remained inoperative.

The problem was, however, brought sharply into focus in December 1880, when the Manitoba Legislature passed an Act extending the boundaries of that province. This Act was confirmed by the Federal Parliament on March 21, 1881, by 44 Vict. Cap. 14. It was not, however, confirmed by the province of Ontario, for the extension of Manitoba eastward was to the "westerly limits of Ontario", which, in Canada's view as well as Manitoba's, followed the meridian of the confluence of the Ohio and the Mississippi. Had Ontario agreed to the Manitoba Boundary Act, it might have been interpreted as meaning that she relinquished all claim to the "Disputed Territory". Manitoba had very practical reasons for wanting her eastern boundary "to correspond with the line marked as the west boundary of Ontario, near the eighty-ninth meridian of west longitude" (37). She wished to be able to supply the "prairie portions" of the province with the timber of the eastern portion and also to obtain a port on Lake Superior (37). Meanwhile, uncertainty and confusion was reported from the area in dispute. In 1881, the stipendiary magistrate appointed by Ontario to exercise jurisdiction there, said:

"You can have but little conception of the difficulties and disappointment [the explorers and miners] have met with here. They have expended all their money in exploring and in surveys, expecting an early return for their investment and toil, which they felt sure they would if the boundary question was settled, so that deeds could be procured for their locations. Without a title nothing can be done with mining capitalists, who require to have an undisputed title to the lands in which they risk their money. The delay . . . in settling the question of the boundary will ruin many, and they will be driven from the locality never to return, causing loss to the merchants and others who have made advances . . . There is no civil court to collect debts, no land agent to locate settlers, no registry office to record deeds, no timber agent to protect the forest. There are timber locations to be had, but there is no security for the expense of exploring and surveying them . . ." (125, p. 453).

Clearly the matter had to be settled, and it was finally agreed to submit the case to the Judicial Committee of the Privy Council for a definite decision. In 1884, the Committee upheld the award made in 1878, which was described by the Canada (Ontario Boundary) Act, 1889, as follows:

"Commencing at the point where the international boundary between the United States of America and Canada strikes the western shores of Lake Superior, thence westerly along the said boundary to the north-west angle of the Lake of the Woods, thence along the line drawn due north until it strikes the middle line of the course of the river discharging the waters of the lake called Lake Seul or the Lonely Lake, whether above or below its confluence with the stream flowing from the Lake of the Woods towards Lake Winnipeg, and thence proceeding eastward from the point at which the before-mentioned line strikes the middle line of the course of the river last aforesaid, along the middle line of the course of the same river (whether called by the name of the English River or, as to the part below the confluence, by the name of the River Winnipeg) up to Lake Seul or the Lonely Lake, and thence along the middle line of Lake Seul or Lonely Lake to the head of that lake, and thence by a straight line to the nearest point of the middle line of the waters of Lake St. Joseph, and thence along the middle line until it reaches the foot or outlet of that lake, and thence along the middle line of the river by which the waters of Lake St. Joseph discharge themselves to the shore of the part of Hudson's Bay commonly known as James Bay, and thence south-easterly following upon the said shore to a point where a line drawn due north from the head of Lake Temiscamingue would strike it, and thence due south along the said line to the head of the said lake, and thence through the middle channel of the said lake into the Ottawa River, and thence descending along the middle of the main channel of the said river to the intersection by the prolongation of the western limits of the Seigneurie of Rigaud, such mid-channel being indicated on the map of the Ottawa Ship Canal Survey made by Walter Shanly, C.E., and approved by Order of the Governor General in Council, dated the twenty-first July, one thousand eight hundred and eighty six; and thence southerly, following the said westerly boundary of the Seigneurie Rigaud to the south-west angle of the said Seigneurie, and then southerly along the western boundary of the augmentation of the Township of Newton to the north-west angle of the Seigneurie of Longueuil, and thence south-easterly along the south-western boundary of said Seigneurie of New Longueuil to the stone boundary of the north bank of the Lake St. Francis, at the cove west of Point au Baudet, such line from the Ottawa River to Lake St. Francis being as indicated on a plan of the line of boundary between Upper and Lower Canada, made in accordance with the Act 23 Victoria, chapter 21" (185).

This description is noteworthy also in that it amplifies and corrects the description of the boundary between Upper and Lower Canada made in 1791. The main clarification is that the boundary shall run through the middle channel of Lake Timiskaming and the middle of the main channel of the Ottawa River, points that were raised in the draft of the Constitutional Bill of 1791 but dropped from the Order in Council following the Constitutional Act. The correction concerns the boundary around the Seigniories of Rigaud and New Longueuil, to which attention has been previously drawn[1].

THE LIMITS OF QUEBEC

The outstanding problems with regard to the boundaries of the province of Quebec in 1867 were somewhat similar to those of Ontario. The boundary on the west was clear enough, but the limits on the north and east were vague.

The Provincial Government of Quebec appears to have taken these problems up at about the time that the Judicial Committee of the Imperial Privy Council upheld the 1878 "Award" to Ontario, when they appointed two select com-

[1] Chapter III.

mittees to consider the question of the northern and northwestern limits of the province. They concluded that although the 52nd degree of north latitude was the northern boundary it would be better to select a boundary that followed the physical features of the landscape in the neighbourhood of this parallel. As with Ontario, Quebec extended as far north as the Hudson's Bay Company's territories, whose limits had been established for Ontario in 1889, according to those that the company had itself been willing to accept in 1700. On the east coast of Hudson Bay, this had been Ruperts River, but the company was later asked to state whether it would consent to a reduction to latitude 52½ degrees north, if the French refused to accept this, and the company, on January 29, 1701, agreed to accept Eastmain River (then called the Canuse), latitude 52°14′ N., as the boundary. Consequently, since 1867, Quebec had some claim to extend as far north as this line.

After the passing of the Canada (Ontario Boundary) Act of 1889, Quebec pressed the matter of the determination of its boundaries more vigorously. The Lieutenant-Governor of Quebec pointed out to the Federal Government that a boundary following 52 degrees north latitude would be entirely "artificial" and would run for about 925 miles through almost inaccessible wilderness. It would be difficult to lay out, quite apart from the expense, which he estimated to be about $1,000,000. Yet only a few miles to the north a "natural" boundary existed that could follow Eastmain River for 420 miles and Hamilton River to the limits of Labrador, leaving some 160 miles only between the headwaters of the Eastmain and Hamilton to follow an imaginary line. Furthermore, it was maintained that as Ontario had been awarded an additional 108,925 square miles of territory and a "natural" boundary, Quebec was entitled to a similar award, even if only in partial compensation for "that portion of New France annexed to Newfoundland". A boundary such as proposed would achieve this, whereas a boundary that followed the 52nd parallel would give Quebec 62,800 square miles only.

Whether it fully agreed with all Quebec's arguments or not, the Government of Canada raised no objections with regard to the general location of the boundary, but was dubious about detail. It felt that neither government had enough information to deal definitely with the matter. Notwithstanding the 1889 award to Ontario, it appeared to be by no means certain that a line drawn due north from the head of Lake Timiskaming would intersect the shores of James Bay. Furthermore, the Deputy Minister of the Interior reported that "next to nothing is known about the Eastmain but, this much is certain, like every other river, it has several branches and before it could be adopted as a boundary it would be necessary to determine which of these branches is the Eastmain River". The same was true of Hamilton River, and it was feared that these rivers might prove to rise far to the north of latitude 52 degrees north and hence give Quebec far more territory than was intended. Exploratory surveys of the proposed boundary area were, therefore, made by the Department of the Interior, and in 1890 Ogilvie determined that the due north line from Lake Temiscaming would meet James Bay. As a result of A. P. Low's investigations from 1892 to 1894, he found that 20 miles from the coast the Eastmain branched, and he was at first unable to determine which was the main branch. Three hundred miles from the coast, the river divided again. However, by 1895 the Dominion Surveyor General was in a position to report that there was sufficient information to describe a well-defined line for the northern boundary of Quebec. It was found possible to follow rivers and lakes except for a distance of about 175 miles between Patamisk Lake and Ashuanipi River. Here, it was suggested, the boundary should follow the 53rd parallel of latitude. Some consideration was given to the use of a watershed line in its place, but although the watershed line was desirable from some points of view, it would be difficult to determine, particularly as it was known that several lakes in the area discharged in two directions. The advantage of having the boundary on an even parallel of latitude enabled any point on it to be easily and instrumentally fixed without the necessity of ascertaining the precise latitude of Patamisk Lake in the first place.

Ultimately the Quebec Legislature agreed to this boundary, and although this was regarded by some (44) as going further than the legal limits, the Parliament of Canada concurred, and in 1898 the northern and eastern boundaries of the province of Quebec were defined as follows:

"Commencing at the head of Lake Temiscamingue, thence along the eastern boundary of the province of Ontario due north to the shore of the part of Hudson Bay commonly known as James Bay, and thence north-easterly following up the said shore to the mouth of the East Main River, and thence easterly ascending along the middle of the said river up to the confluence of the branch thereof flowing from Patamisk Lake, and thence ascending along the middle of the said branch up to Patamisk Lake, and thence along the middle of the said lake to the most northerly point thereof, the said point being about fifteen miles south from the Hudson's Bay Company's post on Lake Nichigun, and approximately in latitude fifty-two degrees fifty-five minutes north, and longitude seventy degrees forty-two minutes west of Greenwich; thence due east along the parallel of latitude of the said point to the intersection of the river discharging the waters of Lake Ashuanipi, which river is known under the names of Hamilton or Ashuanipi or Great Esquimaux River, and thence descending along the middle of the said river through Menihek, Marble, Astray and Dyke Lakes to the most southerly outlet of Dyke Lake, and thence along the middle of the said outlet to Birch Lake, and thence along the middle of Birch and Sandgirt Lakes to the most southerly outlet of Sandgirt Lake, and thence along the middle of the southern channel of the Hamilton River to Flour Lake, and thence along the middle of Flour Lake to its outlet, and thence along the middle of the Hamilton River to the Bay du Rigolet or Hamilton Inlet, and thence easterly along the middle of the said bay or inlet until it strikes the westerly boundary of the territory under the jurisdiction of Newfoundland, and thence southerly along the said boundary to the point where it strikes the north shore of the Ance Sablon, in the Gulf of St. Lawrence" (172).

In a draft suggestion made by the Geological Survey of Canada on the location of this boundary the concluding phrase read ". . . along the main channel of Hamilton River to its mouth" (44). Recognizing that this ignored Newfoundland's possible claims along the coast, this phrase was modified, but was still without precision as far as Labrador's boundary was concerned. Its determination depended upon the documents awarding the coast of Labrador to Newfoundland, the last of which was the Newfoundland Act of 1825.

Just as Ontario's western boundary depended upon an interpretation of various documents issued since 1763, so Quebec's eastern boundary depended upon an interpretation of documents of a similar nature that also stemmed from the Treaty of Paris. But Quebec's eastern boundary was not an interprovincial matter, as Ontario's western boundary had been. Quebec's eastern boundary happened to be an international boundary between Canada and Newfoundland, and it remained an international dispute until the Imperial Privy Council decision of 1927, the events concerned with which have already been discussed[1]. There was some dissatisfaction in the province of Quebec over the decision, however, which became more vocal after Newfoundland joined Canada in 1949 (96) and the "Labrador boundary" became an interprovincial one. Even today, maps published by the province of Quebec do not show the land boundary with the province of Newfoundland: it has, in fact, never been surveyed and demarcated.

But long before the change in Newfoundland's status occurred, there were other boundary problems to be faced by the Government of Canada, which concerned the areas not included in any of the provinces.

---

[1] Chapter IV.

CHAPTER VI

THE "UNORGANIZED" NORTHWEST

Apart from the problems with regard to the precise limits of the provinces of Ontario and Quebec, that Canada as a whole had inherited, she also inherited the problem of the creation of administrative units within the territory formerly controlled by the Hudson's Bay Company, when she acquired Rupert's Land and the Northwest Territories in 1870. The problems related to the creation of the administrative units were of a different nature from those mentioned in the previous chapter, owing to the fact that the establishment of the boundaries was not primarily based on historical documents and treaties.

The British Government's decision with regard to the future of the Hudson's Bay Company's territory was based on the recommendation of the Select Committee of its House of Commons of 1857 and on the reports of Captain John Palliser's western explorations of 1857-60. But in 1870, when the Government of Canada acquired the title to thousands of square miles of territory, the area contained a population of only 48,000 (50, p. 1027), the information on its topography, soil, and climatic conditions was very vague, and there were practically no reliable data or statistics on record. Palliser's report had not been strikingly optimistic. Parts of the west he considered to be by no means suited to settlement (51, p. 9) and, in his opinion, the time had forever gone by for securing a line of communication from Canada to the Pacific exclusively in British territory. "The unfortunate choice of an astronomical boundary", he said, "has completely isolated the Central American possessions of Great Britain from Canada in the east, and has also almost debarred them from any eligible access from the Pacific Coast on the west" (191, p. 16), a conclusion that is reminiscent of the fears that the United States-New Brunswick boundary would sever easy communication between the Maritimes and the St. Lawrence in 1784. So that in spite of Sir John A. Macdonald's words that the government had one great country before them to do with as they liked (38, col. 874), its established southern boundary was the first fact of its political geography that had to be faced.

EARLY BOUNDARY PROBLEMS IN THE TERRITORIES

How did the Hudson's Bay Company administer this huge territory? The truth is that it was not primarily concerned with administration *per se*, but with the development of the fur trade. However, this in itself demanded organization and the company, therefore, divided British North America into four great departments. The Northern Department embraced the area between the United States boundary to the south, the unknown Arctic on the north, Hudson Bay on the east, and the Rocky Mountains on the west. The Southern Department extended "from James Bay southward to the provinces of Upper and Lower Canada and east to include East Main, the eastern coast of Hudson Bay". The Montreal Department covered "the Company's business in Upper and Lower Canada, the King's Posts and, later, Labrador"; and the Columbia Department covered the valley of the Columbia River, and, after 1825, the Canadian Pacific slope called New Caledonia (73, pp. 23, 24).

These departments were subdivided into districts, the boundaries of which usually approximated to watersheds, as the waterways were the arteries of communication and trade in the fur trade period. But it was not the

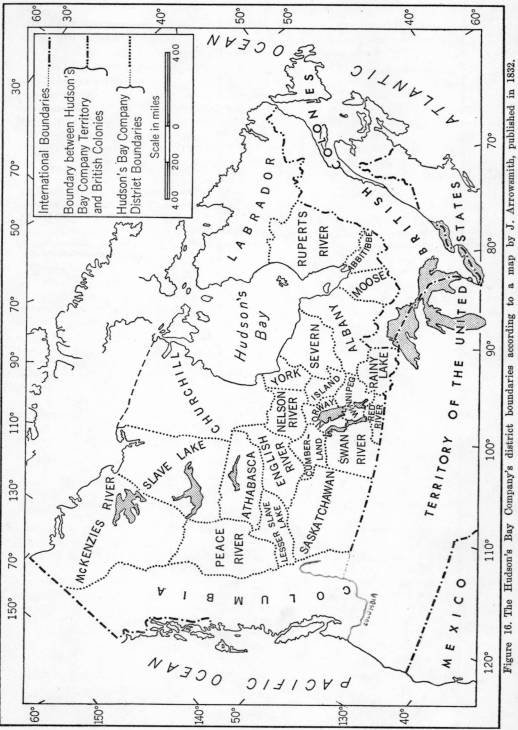

Figure 16. The Hudson's Bay Company's district boundaries according to a map by J. Arrowsmith, published in 1832.

general practice to set exact geographic limits for fur-trade districts. Even the fur-traders themselves did not agree on the boundaries of such districts, or even their numbers, with the result that their limits had little direct influence on official boundary descriptions (82, pp. 269-70).

The government and the company, of course, occupied diametrically opposite positions. The company was not interested in settlement—it was in fact, if anything, opposed to it. To the government, on the other hand, settlement was vital to the building of a nation, and settlement meant surveys. Its primary consideration, therefore, was to devise a system under which the country could be rapidly and accurately subdivided into land holdings and which would forestall the confusion that would follow large-scale immigration into unsurveyed territory. As a result, a system of surveys was approved by Order in Council more than a year before the transfer of the territories (46, p. 31).

The lines resulting from these surveys were the first formal boundaries in the "unorganized" Northwest Territories, but they did not constitute boundaries with the functions under discussion here. But with rapid immigration and land settlement new governments were necessitated. There were several ways in which "unorganized territory" could be "organized". Separate provinces could be created out of "unorganized territory" or parts of the "unorganized territory" could be included in an adjacent province, merely by extending the boundaries of the province. Alternatively the "unorganized territory" could be divided into tracts and each tract could then be given limited jurisdiction over its own affairs under the over-all jurisdiction of an administrative centre in a neighbouring province or under administration controlled completely from Ottawa.

THE CREATION OF MANITOBA

The creation of the province of Manitoba arose out of the settlements established in the Red River Valley by Lord Selkirk. The area that Selkirk selected for settlement in 1811 and subsequently established as Assiniboia included the bed of glacial Lake Agassiz. In 1834, however, the settlement reverted to the Hudson's Bay Company and "the boundaries were changed from the meticulous details of Selkirk's grant to a circular tract with a radius of fifty miles from Fort Garry" (120, p. 209). As created by the Dominion Act of 1870 (169), the province of Manitoba did not quite double this area, as its boundaries were the parallels of north latitude 49° and 50°30' and the meridians of west longitude 96° to 99°, and hence covered about 14,340 square miles. But the boundaries so defined did not correspond with the Dominion Lands System of surveys, and, consequently, in 1877, in order to facilitate the correct registration of land titles in Manitoba and the adjoining parts of Keewatin and the Northwest Territories, the provincial boundaries were re-described according to the Dominion Lands System (171). This procedure did not alter the total area of Manitoba, but did cause the eastern and western boundaries to be moved westward about 5 miles.

A Lieutenant-Governor was appointed for the remainder of the unorganized territory and, as settlement increased, his powers were extended and his advisory body enlarged. But it was soon clear that even this did not provide adequate machinery for the proper administration of the area. In 1876 a plan for the creation of four provinces between Manitoba and British Columbia was prepared at the request of the Minister of the Interior, but was not proceeded with, probably because it was considered premature. The greatest inconvenience was felt where settlement was heaviest—immediately west and east of the boundaries of Manitoba; the eastern area was dealt with first.

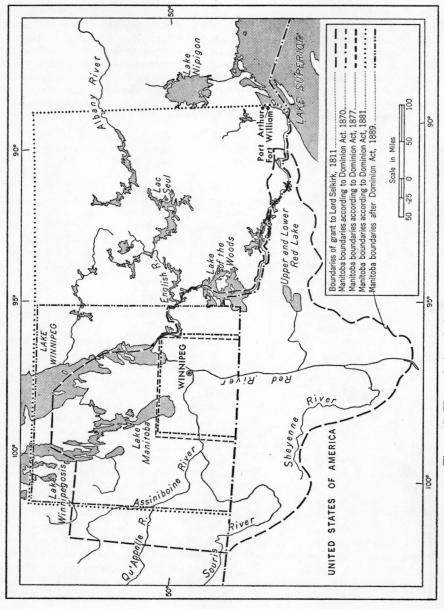

Figure 17. The evolution of the boundaries of Manitoba, 1811-1889.

THE CREATION OF KEEWATIN

It has already been pointed out that the western and northern boundaries of Ontario were in dispute almost as soon as the Dominion of Canada was created. In order to provide for government in the general area west of Ontario, a large portion of the Northwest Territories, covering about 395,000 square miles, was detached and set apart as a separate district under the name of the District of Keewatin on October 7, 1876, by virtue of the proclamation of the Keewatin Act (170). The Act was intended to be temporary in character, being merely intended to give good government to the area north and east of Manitoba and west of Ontario, and read as follows:

"Whereas it is expedient, pending the settlement of the western boundary of Ontario, to create a separate Territory of the Eastern part of the Northwest Territories: Therefore, Her Majesty, by and with the advice and consent of the Senate and House of Commons of Canada, enacts as follows:

1. All that portion of the Northwest Territories, bounded as follows, that is to say:

Beginning at the westerly boundary of the Province of Ontario, on the international boundary line dividing Canada from the United States of America; then westerly, following upon the said international boundary line, to the easterly boundary of the Province of Manitoba; thence due north, along the said easterly boundary of Manitoba, to the north-east angle of the said province; thence due west, on the north boundary of said Province, to the intersection by the said boundary of the westerly shore of Lake Manitoba; thence northerly, following the westerly shore of the said lake, to the easterly terminus thereof of the Portage connecting the southerly end of Lake Winnipegosis with the said Lake Manitoba, known as "The Meadow Portage"; thence westerly, following upon the trail of the said portage, to the westerly terminus of the same, being on the easterly shore of the said Lake Winnipegosis; thence northerly, following the line of the said easterly shore of the said lake to the southerly end of the portage leading from the head of the said lake into "Cedar Lake", known as the "Cedar" or "Mossy Portage"; thence northerly, following the trail of the said portage, to the north end of the same on the shore of Cedar Lake; thence due north, to the northerly limits of Canada; thence easterly following upon the said northerly limits of Canada, to the northerly extremity of Hudson's Bay; thence southerly, following upon the westerly shore of the said Hudson's Bay, to the point where it would be intersected by a line drawn due north from the place of beginning, and thence due south, on the said line last mentioned, to the said place of beginning; shall be, and is hereby set apart as a separate district of the said Northwest Territories by the name of the District of Keewatin" (170).

It will be recalled[1] that in 1874 the longitude of the most easterly point of Hunter's Island (long. 90°58′ W. approx.) had been agreed upon as the provisional western boundary of Ontario. This then must have been the eastern boundary of Keewatin at the time of its creation, although its permanent position was always in doubt until the question of the boundary between Ontario and Manitoba was settled in 1889.

The Lieutenant-Governor of Manitoba became Lieutenant-Governor of the new District of Keewatin, with a council of six persons to aid in the administration of the affairs of Keewatin. Their services were soon called upon when it was discovered, shortly before the district was officially proclaimed, that an epidemic of smallpox had been in existence for some months on the west side of Lake Winnipeg among the Icelanders who had settled there during 1875 and the summer of 1876 (121). Before it was realized that the disease was smallpox, it had spread among the Indians in the vicinity. Consequently, on November 31, 1876, the six members of the Council of Keewatin were named as a Board of Health for the district. When this Board was organized, the spread of smallpox throughout Keewatin, Manitoba, and the Northwest Territories seemed inevitable, and the fact that the disease was localized and confined to comparatively narrow limits was due to the energy of the Board of Health and its officers (140, p. VIII), which at least demonstrated the need for organized government in the area.

---

[1] See Chapter V.

PROBLEMS FARTHER WEST

At the same time as Keewatin was created, a Mounted Police post on Swan River, popularly known as Fort Livingstone, became the administrative centre for what remained of the Northwest Territories; in 1878, it was removed farther west, to Battleford. All transactions in real property had to be recorded in the office of the Registrar for the Northwest Territories there, and the obvious inconveniences of such an arrangement ultimately caused complaints from the settlers, so in 1880 an Order in Council was passed erecting the Turtle Mountain, Little Saskatchewan, Touchwood Hills, and Prince Albert sections into registration districts (141, p. IV). The influx of population into these areas also raised the question of the franchise, so in the same year three electoral districts were created—two adjoining Manitoba on the west, and one known as the Prince Albert Settlement. But the residents of the first two areas, at least, were not satisfied with these developments. They had, on various occasions, expressed a desire to be incorporated into the province of Manitoba, which they contended, was "too circumscribed" (141, p. IV), and on July 1, 1881, by Dominion Act, the boundaries of Manitoba were extended so as to become

"On the south the International boundary, on the west the centre of the road allowance between the twenty-ninth and thirtieth ranges west of the Principal meridian as surveyed in the Dominion Lands Survey System; on the north the centre of the road allowance along the twelfth base line of the Dominion Lands Survey System; on the east the easterly limit of the District of Keewatin. . . .that is, the westerly boundary of the Province of Ontario" (136, p. 3).

It thus included a considerable proportion of the then settled districts of the Territories and relieved the Territorial Government of the supervision of the municipal and educational affairs of such centres of population as the Little Saskatchewan, Rapid City, Birtle, Birdtail Creek, and Turtle Mountain (142, p. V).

But meantime, settlement continued to increase in the Northwest Territories. The rate of development was accelerated by the construction of the Canadian Pacific Railway, which was completed in 1885. In 1882, by an Order in Council, the area south of the thirty-second correction line of the Dominion Lands System; west of Athabasca and Slave Rivers and the line between the tenth and eleventh ranges of Dominion Lands townships west of the fourth initial meridian; and south of the eighteenth correction line of the Dominion Lands System (154, pp. 39, 40) was divided into the provisional districts of Assiniboia, Saskatchewan, Athabaska, and Alberta, to be governed by a Lieutenant-Governor with his capital at Regina, Saskatchewan. These districts were created for federal, administrative, and postal purposes and were rarely referred to in the local legislature at Regina. Nevertheless, it is instructive to examine the geographical setting of the new boundaries. First of all, the northern boundary of the area divided into provisional districts was approximately 60°N., west of $111\frac{1}{2}$°W., and 55°N. east of that meridian (Figure 21) and the position of this line interestingly reflects the fact that the pattern of settlement in the area was already being affected by the factors of the physical environment. These were the western limits of the Canadian Shield and what was thought, at that time, to be the position of the 60°F. mean summer isotherm, which would have represented the northern limit of the climatic and soil conditions that are suitable for mid-latitude agriculture. Furthermore, it must be remembered that the early settlers in western Canada avoided the open grasslands and took up land in the wooded areas and river valleys. Each of the new provisional districts included a major river valley or part of one—the Assiniboine, Qu'Appelle, and South Saskatchewan in Assiniboia; the North Saskatchewan in Saskatchewan and Alberta; and the Athabasca and Peace in Athabaska. In addition, before the coming of the railway there were considerable settlements of half-breeds at Edmonton, Prince Albert, and Battleford (107, p. 53). The first of these was included in Alberta and the other two in Saskatchewan. The territorial capital had already migrated northwestward along the "park belt" and was now in the grasslands to the south at Regina. It was presumably because this area had different physical characteristics that it was set apart as Assiniboia. Even after the trans-Canada railway had been completed, the map of population distribution for 1886 (107, p. 48) shows clearly an east-west break between the districts of Saskatchewan and Assiniboia; the break roughly corresponds with the sparsely populated areas of the Bear, Allan, Touchwood, and Beaver Hills, a factor that was probably taken into account in locating the provisional boundary.

The boundaries of the District of Saskatchewan were described as follows:

". . . . to be bounded on the south by the districts of Assiniboia and Manitoba; on the east by Lake Winnipeg and the Nelson River flowing therefrom into Hudson Bay; on the north by the eighteenth correction line of the Dominion land survey system, and on the west by the line of that system dividing the tenth and eleventh ranges of townships numbered from the fourth initial meridian" (154, p. 39).

This description is given in detail, not only to serve as an example of how the provisional districts were described but also to show that in the case of Saskatchewan the boundaries overlapped those assigned to the District of Keewatin in 1876. The intention was probably to include the settlements that had sprung up in the "overlapping portion" in the provisional district of Saskatchewan, because they were economically and socially akin to the other settlements in that district rather than to those in Keewatin. By an Order in Council dated May 7, 1886, the "overlapping portion"—that part of Keewatin lying between Manitoba and the eighteenth correction line and west of Nelson River —was re-annexed to the Northwest Territories in order to become properly a part of Saskatchewan.

But there were still unorganized and unnamed districts of the Northwest Territories north of those created in 1882, and in 1895, for the further convenience of settlers and for postal purposes, the Minister of the Interior recommended that four such districts be established and named Ungava, Franklin, Mackenzie, and Yukon, and that changes be made in the boundaries of the districts of Athabaska and Keewatin so as to enlarge their areas.

The first five of these proposals took account of the increase in population of various parts of the Northwest Territories by extending Athabaska eastwards so as to include the area north of Saskatchewan, east of Keewatin, and south of the 60th parallel[1], and by dividing all of the remainder of the territories into districts. Keewatin itself, however, had been something of a special problem.

THE REORGANIZATION OF KEEWATIN

It will be recalled that, by 1889, the Ontario-Manitoba boundary dispute had been settled. The decision that gave to the province of Ontario the territory south of Albany River and as far west as Lake of the Woods limited the District of Keewatin to the territory lying directly north of the province of Manitoba, and fixed its eastern boundary at the longitude of a line running north from the western boundary of the province of Ontario. This left the status of the area between Keewatin and James Bay and north of Ontario in doubt, and when, prior to 1895, the creation of new districts in the territories

[1] Actually, the thirty-second correction line of the Dominion Lands System, which was almost 60 degrees north.

was being contemplated, this area was something of a problem. There seemed to be little doubt that the area should be associated with Keewatin, but the problem was how to rearrange the boundaries of Keewatin so as to effect this.

The Lieutenant-Governor of Keewatin recommended the addition of this area to Keewatin, as in his view, it was accessible only through Hudson's Straits or by the rivers that flow into Lake Winnipeg, and could, therefore, be effectively governed only in the manner in which the District of Keewatin was governed.

Two other proposals were considered by the Federal Government in 1892. One was that the area proposed by the Lieutenant-Governor should be limited on the north and west by Lake Winnipeg and Churchill River. The reason given for this was that such boundaries would give a territory within the jurisdiction of the Lieutenant-Governor of Manitoba, who was also the Lieutenant-Governor of Keewatin, within which the greater part of the population then in Keewatin was to be found, and which could be administered with convenience from Winnipeg because of the comparative facility with which it could be reached by water from that point via Red River and Lake Winnipeg and its tributaries. However, the boundaries of Keewatin according to this proposal would have been rather irregular and would involve a lengthy description. Because of this, a third proposal suggested the 99th meridian west as the western boundary instead of the longitude of the Mossy Portage meridian.

However, it was by no means universally agreed that the area under consideration was not already part of Manitoba, for the boundaries of that province had, in 1881, been extended to " the westerly limits of Ontario". If, after the Canada (Ontario Boundary) Act of 1889, the word "westerly" was interpreted broadly so as to include the *northwestern* boundaries of Ontario, then it could be argued that the "doubtful area" was part of Manitoba (39). In these circumstances, no immediate action was taken. Two more boundary proposals were then made. One was to the effect that the eastern limit of Keewatin should be the prolongation, due north, of the dividing line between Ontario and Quebec. The other was that the western boundary of Keewatin should be the 2nd meridian of the Dominion Lands System (102 degrees west longitude), which would have meant re-attaching part of the district of Saskatchewan to Manitoba. This was not recommended, as it was an "imaginary" line, and a "geographical" boundary like Lake Manitoba and Nelson River was preferable. Furthermore, it would not have "improved" the map, as it would have left in the District of Keewatin a narrow wedge of the Porcupine Hills country "jammed in between Saskatchewan and Manitoba".

The ultimate recommendation chose a western boundary between the 2nd meridian and 99 degrees west, namely, 100 degrees west, and included in Keewatin the area between Hudson Bay and the northerly boundary of Ontario.

These and the other changes in territorial boundaries suggested by the Minister were made by Order in Council in 1895; the Order also recommended that the Keewatin boundary changes be authorized by an Act of Parliament. This, however, was not done, as discrepancies were found to exist in the descriptions of the district boundaries, and in 1897 there was promulgated a further Order in Council cancelling the Order of 1895 and previous orders and approving the recommendations of the Minister of the Interior that the districts of Assiniboia, Saskatchewan, and Athabaska remain as they were established in 1895; it also provided that the boundaries of Ungava, Keewatin, Mackenzie, Yukon, and Franklin should be slightly changed[1] according to a given description and map. These changes in boundaries were made mainly to ensure that all the islands between 141 degrees west and Davis Strait were included in one or

---

[1] See Chapter IV.

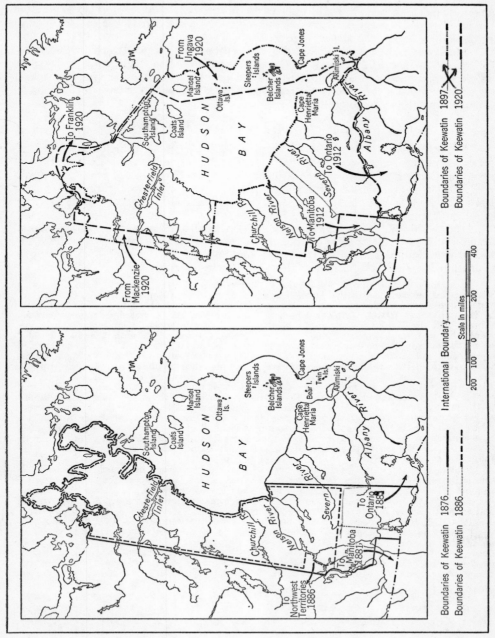

Figure 18. The evolution of the boundaries of Keewatin.

other of the provisional districts, which the Order in Council of 1895 had failed to do. Ungava, Franklin, and Keewatin were also so defined as to embrace the whole of Hudson Bay and Strait. But legislation regarding these changes was never introduced, and it would appear, therefore, that the districts, except in so far as they were authorized by the subsequently cancelled Order in Council of 1882, had no legal existence (17, p. 22).

Meanwhile an Act of 1887 had given representation at Ottawa to the territories, and an Act of 1888 had set up an elected territorial legislature at Regina. These developments clearly pointed toward provincial status for some, at least, of the territories, but before that stage was reached further developments occurred in the far northwest.

THE CREATION OF YUKON TERRITORY

Reports that that part of the Yukon Valley lying within Canada was of great economic value, particularly in regard to its mineral wealth, had been reaching Ottawa for several years prior to 1886. The mineral was, of course, gold, and the number of miners entering the area increased rapidly. About three hundred were estimated to be in the area in the summer of 1887, and the number increased to thousands after the famous Klondike strike on August 17, 1896. This influx, as has already been pointed out, caused an international boundary situation, but it also demanded an internal adjustment to allow for the proper administration of the area, and in 1897 the District of Yukon was proclaimed a judicial district, with the following boundaries:

"Beginning at the intersection of the 141st meridian of west longitude from Greenwich with a point on the coast of the Arctic Sea, which is approximate north latitude, 69°39′, ... thence due south, on the said meridian .... for a distance of about 650 miles, to a point in latitude about 60°10′ north, at which it will intersect the disputed boundary between Canada and the United States on the North Pacific coast; thence in an easterly direction, along the said undetermined boundary .... to its intersection with the 60th parallel of north latitude; thence due east along the parallel of latitude .... for a distance of about 550 miles, to the Liard River, in approximate longitude 123°30′ west, thence northerly along the middle line of said river, for a distance of about 10 miles till opposite the highest part of the range of mountains which abuts upon the river near the mouth of Black River; thence to follow the summit of said range in a northwesterly direction to the southernmost source of the Peel River; thence to follow northward the summit of the main range of mountains which runs approximately parallel to Peel River; on the west, as far as the intersection of the said range with the 136th meridian; thereafter to run due north to the Arctic Ocean, or to the westernmost channel of the Mackenzie Delta, and along that channel to the Arctic Ocean; thence northwesterly following the windings of the Arctic Coast, ... including Herschel Island, and all other islands which may be situated within three (3) geographical miles, to the place of beginning.

Provided, that in respect to that part of the line, between the Liard River and the southernmost source of the Peel River, the summit to be followed is the watershed summit separating streams entering the Liard River below Black River, or flowing directly into the Mackenzie further north, from streams flowing westward either to the Yukon or to upper branches of the Liard River.

Provided, that in respect to the part of the boundary described as following northward the main range of mountains on the west side of the Peel River, the line shall run along the watershed between streams flowing eastwardly to the Peel River, and those flowing westwardly to branches of the Yukon, Porcupine, etc., except where such watershed shall be more than 20 miles distant from the main stream of the Peel, when the highest range within that distance shall be the boundary" (173).

But it became increasingly clear that it was also necessary to make special provision for the maintenance of law and order in the district because about 90 per cent of the people in the territory were aliens and few of them intended to settle there permanently. Indeed, the intention of many of them was to "make a fortune" and return to their families in other parts of the world (35, p. 859). Consequently, on June 13, 1898, the District of Yukon was constituted a separate Territory with the same boundaries as had been assigned to it when it had been proclaimed a judicial district.

These boundaries are different in character from those assigned to the provisional districts farther south in that in the east they attempt to follow topographical features rather than parallels of latitude and longitude. The very vagueness of their description, however, indicates how little was known of the geography of the region. The intention was to make them largely correspond with the watershed between the Yukon and Mackenzie river systems (40, col. 6747). The reason for this was, presumably, because the gold being mined was alluvial or "stream gold" and as the purpose of the creation of the separate territory was to bring law and order to the mining settlements and activities, the territory had to include all the possible gold mining areas, i.e., Yukon River, its tributaries, and associated waterways. In this respect the boundaries of the Yukon Territory were similar in purpose to the extension of the boundaries of British Columbia to the 120th meridian west and the 60th parallel in 1863. In the case of British Columbia, however, the de-limitation was made purely in terms of latitude and longitude, so as to include all the possible potential alluvial gold areas that existed on both sides of the Pacific Ocean-Arctic Ocean divide. As time went on, and more became known about the area, it was possible to describe the boundaries more simply and accurately so that, at present, they are legally described as follows:

"On the south, by the province of British Columbia and the United States Territory of Alaska; on the west by the said United States Territory of Alaska; on the north, by that part of the Arctic Ocean called Beaufort sea; and on the east by a line beginning at the point of intersection of the left bank of the Liard river, by the northern boundary of the province of British Columbia in approximate longitude 124°16' west of Greenwich; thence northwesterly along the line of the watershed separating the streams flowing into the Liard river below the point of beginning or into the Mackenzie river, from those flowing into the Liard river above the point of beginning, or into the Yukon river, to the line of watershed of the basin of Peel river; thence northerly along the line of water-shed between the Peel and Mackenzie rivers to the sixty-seventh degree of north latitude; thence westerly along the parallel of the sixty-seventh degree of north latitude to the line of watershed between the Peel and Yukon rivers; thence northerly along the said line of watershed to the trail across the portage in McDougall pass between Rat and Bell rivers; thence due north to the northern limit of the Yukon Territory; the said Territory to include the islands within twenty statute miles from the shores of the Beaufort sea as far as the aforesaid due north line from McDougall pass" (182a).

Boundary evolution in the Northwest Territories between 1870 and 1898, therefore, saw two different types of boundaries emerge. The first type was based on lines of the Dominion Lands System—the only type of boundary possible in an area that was being rapidly settled by agriculturalists in a region that lacked marked physical features. The idea of boundaries that approxi-mately followed lines of latitude and longitude was then extended into those parts of the territories that were north of the area of likely agricultural development, partly, it appears now, to uphold Canadian sovereignty in the north. The second type of boundary was basically a watershed one, as exempli-fied in the Yukon Territory.

The boundaries of Keewatin showed a combination of both these features. This reflected the fact that Keewatin was a "bridge" between the two types of economy—that based on agriculture or exploitation of the plains and that based on the more primitive fur trade of the forest and tundra. The fact that the boundaries of Keewatin were changed and amended so many times and as the result of many different suggestions also reflects the "buffer-like" situation of the territory between the older settled areas of the east and the newly developed areas of the west.

The creation of the separate Yukon Territory in the extreme northwest of continental Canada resulted from a remarkable increase in population in that area. But even greater increases of population were occurring in the areas farther south, and emphasized the necessity for additional boundary changes.

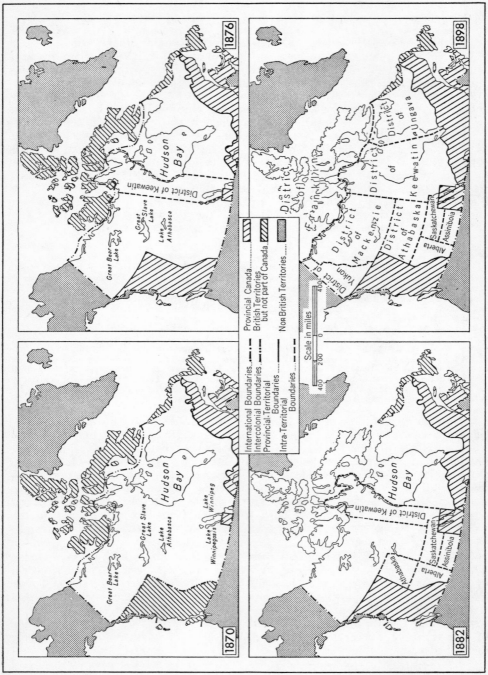

Figure 19. Territorial and intra-territorial boundaries, 1870-1898.

CHAPTER VII

NEW PROVINCES AND RESULTING ADJUSTMENTS

During the period 1897 to 1905, the territories developed very rapidly. In the years immediately following Confederation, the small population had been scattered, and was concentrated chiefly in a few small communities that had grown up about the old trading posts and the new Northwest Mounted Police posts. With the active immigration policy that followed, Manitoba received most of the new Canadians until the Canadian Pacific Railway was constructed in the early 1880s, when population began to spread westward at an unprecedented rate. Immigration was under the control of the Federal Government, but the task of providing for the immigrants by the construction of local works and improvements was the responsibility of the Territorial Government. The problems (mainly financial) created as a result of this gradually became almost insurmountable, and, consequently, the territories began to look forward to provincial status (98, pp. 8, 9).

The various opinions and arguments advanced on this question are of concern here only in so far as they have a bearing on boundary evolution and significance. If the territories, or any parts of them, were to be erected into provinces, what should the boundaries of the latter be?

NEW PROVINCES

Several proposals were put forward regarding the possible boundaries for new provinces. The people of the Territories themselves were by no means unanimous even with respect to the number of provinces, and in the Assembly proposals for one, two, and three provinces all found supporters; there was also a small group that favoured the annexation of a part of the Territories to Manitoba (98, p. 68). The Dominion Government had at times considered four provinces. Each of these proposals will now be examined briefly.

ANNEXATION TO MANITOBA

During the controversy over her eastern boundary, Manitoba had contended that it should be extended westwards to the 2nd meridian of the Dominion Lands System (102 degrees west) and had made repeated requests to the Dominion Government to have this brought about. In 1883 the Executive Council of the Province of Manitoba expressed this desire officially, and so advised Ottawa in 1884. In 1884 a further Order in Council was passed by the Executive Council of Manitoba to the same effect, and this was followed 2 weeks later by a resolution passed by the Legislative Assembly of the province deputing the members of the Executive Council to proceed to Ottawa to procure from the Dominion Government a settlement of what they maintained were their rights to have the boundaries of the province extended. In 1901, the Manitoba Legislature passed a further resolution requesting the extension of the province into adjacent districts that possessed agricultural, commercial, and educational interests "in a great measure common" to its own, and including as much of the territory as might be consistent wtih economical and efficient government (154, p. 9). An even stronger and more lengthy resolution along similar lines was passed by the Legislature in 1902. This resolution contended that it was "of the highest importance" to the province of Manitoba and the Northwest Territories that the former "should be increased by an extension of boundaries so as to embrace and include a portion of the districts of Assiniboia and Saskatchewan and northwards to Hudson Bay" (154, p. 10). Still further resolutions in similar terms were adopted in 1905 and 1906.

Some support for a westward extension of Manitoba had come from Alberta. In 1897 the City Council of Calgary passed a resolution that:

"The material interest and prosperity of the districts would be best promoted and the multiplication of Governments avoided by adding that portion of Assiniboia lying between the Province of Manitoba and the Third meridian to Manitoba and erecting the remainder of Assiniboia, Alberta and Saskatchewan into one Governmental District with Provincial powers."

This was not an entirely disinterested view of Manitoba's case, however, for on March 16, 1901, the *Calgary Albertan* reported the same proposal, with the suggestion that Calgary should become the capital of the new province to the west of Manitoba. The proposal reappeared from time to time, particularly when it was known that a final decision was about to be made. The geographical reasoning followed the argument that the eastern part of the territories was naturally tributary to Manitoba, that the climatic conditions were alike, and the agricultural possibilities very similar, even if Manitoba were extended as far west as Regina (20).

However, most of the inhabitants of the territories were opposed to any annexation. Premier Haultain maintained that the territorial laws were better suited to western conditions than those of Manitoba. Manitoba's municipal system was patterned on that of Ontario, which was not suited to western settlement. The territories had evolved their own local institutions in line with their particular needs, such as the system of local improvement districts, and had not introduced the "cumbersome" and "expensive" system in use in Ontario (98, p. 132).

Manitoba refused to give up, however, and in 1905 a delegation to Ottawa presented the request of a united legislature for an extension of the province's boundaries "as far west as Regina" and northward to include Fort Churchill, Nelson River, and the Territory tributary thereto. They argued that the westward extension would comprise a region whose agricultural conditions were similar to their own, and that they were entitled to an area equal in size to any province about to be formed (98, p. 134).

TWO PROVINCES

A second suggestion was to the effect that two provinces should be erected, divided by a line running east and west along the southern boundary of the District of Saskatchewan, because of the differences in the physical geography between the north and the south. The south, it was maintained, was a flat, treeless prairie, adapted to large farming operations such as grain-growing and ranching, whereas the north was rolling, well watered, and possessing abundant wood and hay, making it suitable for mixed farming and smaller holdings. The dividing line between these conditions, would, it was submitted, coincide with the northern boundary of Assiniboia extended westward to the Rocky Mountains. Furthermore, the north and south would each possess transportation facilities, as the Canadian Pacific and Canadian Northern Railway Companies were each operating transcontinental lines running east and west (98, p. 72).

Other groups in the west (20, 131, 108, 112) advocated two provinces divided by a boundary running north and south. They considered that legislation beneficial to the eastern and northern parts of the Territories, where the raising of cereal crops was practically the sole activity, was injurious to the southwest portions, where cattle and horse ranching prevailed. If they could not have one single province with diversified interests they wanted "complete severance" of the "stock country" of Assiniboia and Alberta and the mixed farming country of northern Alberta from the farming country of Assiniboia and Saskatchewan. The suggestions for the exact location of the dividing line varied only in detail. In order not to divide the range lands, the 105th line of longitude was suggested, or that the line should run east of Swift Current, through Swift Current itself, through Moose Jaw, or "at the most" through Maple Creek.

But in addition to these arguments one must also consider the sectional ambitions of Calgary and Edmonton, both of which desired to be capitals (21).

THREE PROVINCES

A group in Prince Albert advocated three provinces—Assiniboia and the southern part of Alberta (by extending the northern boundary of Assiniboia to the Rockies), northern Alberta and the Peace River country (by extending the western boundary of Saskatchewan to the northern boundary of Athabaska), and Saskatchewan and eastern Athabaska. Such a division, they submitted, would meet the wishes and aspirations of the people, would simplify the question of rivalry over location of the capital, and would maintain a balance among the various provinces (98, p. 73).

ONE PROVINCE

The idea of a single political unit between the Great Lakes and British Columbia was current long before Confederation. As a result of his exploratory surveys, Captain Palliser "felt decidedly in favour" of a single British colony from British Columbia up to, and including, the Red River settlement. He suggested that its southern boundary should be the 49th Parallel from the "east shore of the Lake of the Woods, to where it meets the crest of the Rocky Mountains". The remaining boundaries should commence at the 49th Parallel on the western shore of Lake of the Woods, and follow the western margin of that lake "to the watercourse which unites with Lake Winnipeg, from thence extending around the eastern shore of Lake Winnipeg, and following the water course of that lake to the 54th parallel of N. lat. in long. 98° W."; thence along this parallel to its intersection with the crest of the Rocky Mountains (51, p. 4). He estimated that the area of such a unit would be 240,000 square miles, which in the light of the areas of the provinces of today was not unreasonable.

The Premier of the Territories always favoured the erection of one strong united province, and believed that the desire for division was simply founded upon the ambition of certain cities to become provincial capitals. He held that there was no point in the Territories, however remote, which, with the aid of telegraph, telephone, and railway, could not be administered by one western government. He could not recall a single occasion when there had been any conflict of interest upon any question raised in the Legislature, and although admitting that geographical diversity existed, felt that the situation merely called for diversity of treatment. For "no one could map out a province, however small, which would not have diversity of interests" (98, p. 74).

In a draft bill that placed the views of the Executive Council of the Territories before the Federal Government "one province" was envisaged, to be made up of the Districts of Assiniboia, Saskatchewan, Alberta, and that part of the District of Athabaska lying to the south of the 57th parallel of north latitude (98, p. 38).

FOUR PROVINCES

As has been mentioned, the Dominion Government had at times considered the erection of the Northwest Territories into four provinces. The various proposals are worth presenting because of the light they shed on the principles of boundary-making that Ottawa considered important and also because they provide a better understanding of the decision ultimately reached.

In 1876 the Deputy Minister of the Interior had informally submitted a plan for the division of the Northwest Territories into provinces, which was based upon the projected route of the Canadian Pacific Railway (Figure 22f). This route passed north of Fort Pelly and the Elbow of Saskatchewan River and continued westerly to the Rockies via Edmonton. The suggested arrangement of provinces would have enabled each to share equally the advantages of the railway.

The abandonment of this route in favour of one passing south of Fort Ellice and Qu'Appelle and towards the Rockies by the valley of the south branch of the Saskatchewan resulted in a second plan of division (Figure 22e) in 1881. The suggestion was framed with the object in mind of reasonable areas for the different provinces, of the equalization of such areas as far as practicable, and of securing to each province, as nearly as possible, an equal share of the natural resources of the Territories, including all those advantages which could be foreseen.

The areas of two of these suggested provinces were estimated at 95,000 square miles each, and the areas of the other two at 100,000 square miles and 122,000 square miles respectively. It was recognized that provinces three and four were smaller than one and two, but it was felt that this was more than counterbalanced in province two by the existence of a very considerable amount of "unavailable" land, made up of mountains, and the swampy country said to exist around the headwaters of Athabasca River, and in province one by the large tract of swampy country said to exist north of Lesser Slave Lake, and between Athabasca and Peace Rivers.

The known natural resources of each of these areas were also examined and described, and the whole area was considered in relation to the position of the summer isotherm of 60°F., as it was known at that time, which was regarded as the northerly limit of the area climatically suited to the growing of cereals to advantage.

THE DECISION

In 1905, Sir Wilfred Laurier introduced legislation providing for the creation of two provinces. Manitoba's request to be extended westward so as to include a strip of the Northwest Territories had been refused on the grounds that it would be against the wishes of those occupying the strip in question, which had become a settled area with defined and well-established institutions, occupied by people who had, in the main, resided there for a sufficient length of time to become the owners of the property they occupied (153, p. 8).

Ottawa (41) took the view that the Northwest Territories covered too large an area for a single province. It was also of the opinion that the area north of approximately 60 degrees north and west of Keewatin was "absolutely unfit for agriculture", and that although it possessed indications of mineral wealth, without agriculture there could be little hope of "thick and permanent settlement", and, consequently, stable provincial government. It was the intention, therefore, to give provincial autonomy to that part of the Territories situated between the American boundary and the 60th parallel of north latitude,

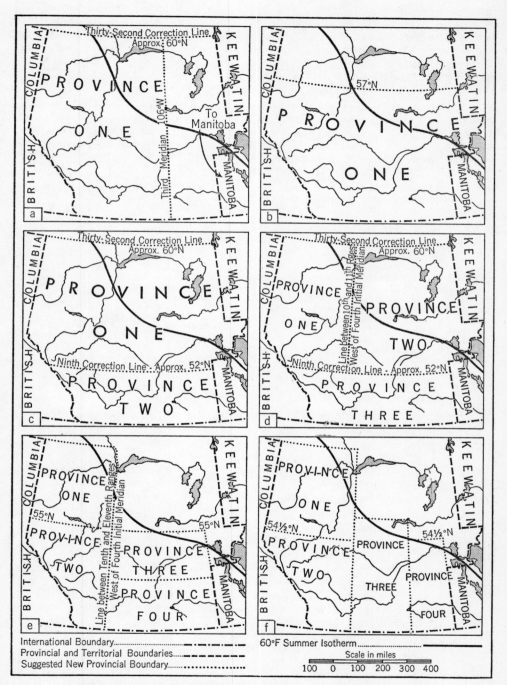

Figure 20. Suggested new provinces in western Canada prior to 1905.

and between British Columbia and Keewatin. This area, comprising 550,345 square miles, was still, in the Federal Government's estimation, too large for a single province, when compared with the other members of Confederation, and, consequently, it was proposed to divide it into two of approximately equal size, by a line running north and south along the 4th meridian (110 degrees west), giving to each of the new provinces an area of about 275,000 square miles and a population of about 250,000.

The first of the new provinces was to be called Alberta and was to have the following boundaries:

"commencing at the intersection of the international boundary dividing Canada from the United States of America by the fourth meridian in the system of Dominion land surveys; thence westerly along the said international boundary to the eastern boundary of the province of British Columbia; thence northerly along the said eastern boundary of the province of British Columbia to the northeast corner of the said province; thence easterly along the parallel of the sixtieth degree of north latitude to the fourth meridian in the system of Dominion lands surveys as the same may be hereafter defined in accordance with the said system; thence southerly along the said fourth meridian to the point of commencement" (175).

The second was to be called Saskatchewan, with the following boundaries:

"commencing at the intersection of the international boundary dividing Canada from the United States of America by the west boundary of the province of Manitoba, thence northerly along the said west boundary of the province of Manitoba; to the north-west corner of the said province of Manitoba; thence continuing northerly along the centre of the road allowance between the twenty-ninth and thirtieth ranges west of the principal meridian in the system of Dominion lands surveys, as the said road allowance may hereafter be defined in accordance with the said system, to the second meridian in the said system of Dominion lands surveys, as the same may hereafter be defined in accordance with the said system; thence northerly along the said second meridian to the sixtieth degree of north latitude; thence westerly along the parallel of the sixtieth degree of north latitude to the fourth meridian in the said system of Dominion lands surveys, as the same may be hereafter defined in accordance with the said system; thence southerly along the said fourth meridian to the said international boundary dividing Canada from the United States of America; thence easterly along the said international boundary to the point of commencement" (176).

There was criticism of the dividing line. Calgary, Medicine Hat, and Macleod all objected to the division of the range country. They maintained (22, 112) that the line should have been farther east so as to take in all the grazing land south of South Saskatchewan River even if north of the river it swerved westward. Both the 105th and 107th meridians were suggested as suitable eastern limits of the range country. The 110th meridian, it was contended, split those interested in the livestock industry, would cause hardship by increasing expenses owing to dealings with "two classes of people", and would be very annoying to the stockmen if the two new provinces adopted different sets of brand and stock laws. While opposing the division of the Territories into two provinces, Premier Haultain likewise held the opinion that the dividing line should be 75 miles farther east. The ranching community of Maple Creek, which found itself within the province of Saskatchewan, was, however, in favour of the 4th meridian.

It must be remembered that by 1901 settlement in the new boundary area had not extended very far north of the 49th Parallel, and the effect of the dividing line was, therefore, felt chiefly in the southern parts of the new provinces. The criticism that it divided the ranching country between Medicine Hat and Swift Current was not groundless. Even modern soil surveys have failed to reveal a better use for this land than extensive grazing, and, topographically, southwestern Saskatchewan differs markedly from southern Saskatchewan farther east. It is doubtful, however, if the division has caused any permanent hardship.

The ultimate decision showed none of the concern for the geography of the country that had been in evidence since 1880, both with regard to the erection of provisional territorial districts and the suggestions for new provinces. As the *Calgary Herald* put it, "the dividing line . . . is wrong, placed there evidently in an arbitrary manner without consideration and without regard to the physical features of the country or its agricultural and grazing qualities" (22). But the Federal Government was well aware of these factors. Indeed, the Department of the Interior prepared a memorandum and a map that showed that the Province of Alberta was neither primarily semi-arid and hence suited only to ranching, nor the Province of Saskatchewan primarily suited only to growing grain (152, p. 5).

BOUNDARY EXTENSIONS

The creation of the provinces of Alberta and Saskatchewan necessitated changes in the boundaries of the Northwest Territories, as the new provinces did not include those parts of the provisional districts of Saskatchewan and Athabaska lying north of the Manitoba boundary.

These either had to remain as separate provisional districts or be incorporated into the District of Keewatin, which was still under the Lieutenant-Governor of Manitoba. The necessary changes were accomplished in three stages. First of all, on the day that the two new provinces were proclaimed (July 20, 1905), an Act amending the "Northwest Territories Act" was passed. This Act declared that the Northwest Territories should comprise Rupert's Land: all of the Northwest Territory except such portions thereof as comprised the provinces of Manitoba, Alberta, and Saskatchewan; the District of Keewatin; and the Yukon Territory. Secondly, 4 days later, an Order in Council was passed by the Dominion Government whereby the whole of the territory comprised within the District of Keewatin was included in the Northwest Territories. Thirdly, by the Act of 1906, the boundaries of the Northwest Territories, as a whole, were redefined.

But the creation of the two "prairie provinces" also intensified the demands of Manitoba, Ontario, and Quebec for a northward extension, now that British Columbia, Alberta, and Saskatchewan all extended to the 60th parallel.

It has already been mentioned, incidentally, that Manitoba's earlier demands for an extension westward also included demands for an extension northward to Hudson Bay. The memorial to this effect, authorized by the Manitoba Legislature in 1905, resulted in a conference between Manitoba government officials and the Prime Minister of Canada, but the latter later stated that the northern extension would be held in abeyance until a conference with the representatives of Ontario, Quebec, Saskatchewan, and Manitoba could take place. At this conference the claims of each of the provinces could be examined (41, cols. 1428-31). Ultimately, however, a conference was held between the Federal Government and those of Saskatchewan, Manitoba, and Ontario only, in November 1906.

THE CLAIMS OF SASKATCHEWAN

Saskatchewan claimed an extension of her boundaries on two counts. In the first place she claimed that her boundaries should be extended eastward so as to include those parts of the Northwest Territories that were formerly part of the provisional districts of Saskatchewan and Athabaska. This claim was based on the fact that this territory was under the control of the administration of the Northwest Territories from its organization until the formation of the Province of Saskatchewan, when it was not included within the area of that province, and on evidence which showed that at least some of its inhabitants wished to be included within the Province of Saskatchewan (154, p. 41).

Secondly, Saskatchewan contended that her boundaries should be extended to the shores of Hudson Bay *as a right* so that the province could have direct water communication with the Atlantic Ocean by way of Hudson Bay and Hudson Strait. The province had already been given some encouragement to think of such an extension as a right by the Prime Minister of Canada (41), and it contended that that part of the Northwest Territories bordering on Hudson Bay and lying between Nelson River and the 60th parallel of latitude should be awarded to it. It was maintained that a "natural" boundary line between the provinces of Saskatchewan and Manitoba would be found in Nelson River and that the awarding to Saskatchewan of the territory north of this river would not interfere with the granting of Manitoba's reasonable request to have her boundaries extended to Hudson Bay as "from the mouth of the Nelson river to where the province of Ontario touches James Bay" there was a coast of several hundred miles with which Manitoba's desire for an extension to the bay could be gratified.

"Further, it is submitted, that there is a vast expanse of territory lying south and east of the Nelson river, being part of the Northwest Territories and containing some 208,000 square miles which is available for the purpose of satisfying Manitoba's demand for increased area. . . . If this entire portion were given to Manitoba, that province would contain an area of over 280,000 square miles, a larger area than possessed by any other province of Canada, except the province of Quebec and the province of British Columbia. Even if the province of Ontario is considered to be entitled to recognition in the distribution of this territory, it is maintained, that there is a sufficient area south and east of the Nelson river to satisfy all legitimate claims for an extension of boundaries both of the province of Manitoba and the province of Ontario" (154, pp. 45-46).

THE CLAIMS OF ONTARIO

Ontario claimed a northward extension merely as a matter of right, although she supported Manitoba's request that her boundaries be extended to Hudson Bay. Ontario then suggested that this northward extension should be made by producing the existing eastern boundary of Manitoba northward until it struck Churchill River, and then following the middle of the channel of that river to its mouth, and that the territory of Manitoba be extended as far north, at least, as the 60th parallel of latitude. For "geographical and other reasons" the remainder of the territory of Keewatin lying east of the suggested eastern boundary of Manitoba, contiguous to Ontario and bounded on the north and east by Hudson Bay and James Bay should be allotted to the province of Ontario (154, p. 33). It was not stated what the geographical and other reasons were.

THE CLAIMS OF MANITOBA

The claims of Manitoba were much more forcefully presented and were supported by much more evidence than in either of the previous cases. The population of the province had increased from 62,260 in 1881 to an estimated 360,000 in 1906, a population in excess of either that of Alberta or Saskatchewan, which had each been given an area of approximately 175,000 square miles more than Manitoba, and it was felt that the province was entitled to increased area so as to enable it to occupy the independent position that was contemplated by the spirit of confederation. For these reasons an increase in area that would place it on a proportionate equality with the other provinces was requested. It was pointed out that in 1881 the Dominion Government had been willing to increase Manitoba's area from 13,500 square miles to 154,000 square miles and that this increase would actually have taken place if it had not been for the later Privy Council decision. For this reason, the area lying west of the proposed Manitoba boundary of 1881, and not given to Ontario by the Privy Council decision, was claimed.

It was also maintained that it was the intention of the Dominion Government, in 1876, at the time of the passage of the Keewatin Act, to ultimately extend the boundaries of Manitoba so as to include a large part of Keewatin, if not the whole of it. In support of this, it was pointed out that for centuries the only means of communication between the Red River settlements and the outside world was through this territory, by way of Hudson Bay. The powers of the Lieutenant-Governor of Manitoba as Lieutenant-Governor of Keewatin from 1876 to 1905, together with other evidence, were adduced to show that Manitoba had always been particularly identified with "Hudson Bay and the intervening territory", which was not true in the case of Ontario. It was further submitted that the development and administration of this intervening territory could best be secured by Manitoba, as the seat of government of Ontario was far removed from the area and, geographically, Manitoba was also in a much better position than the province of Saskatchewan. In any case, both these provinces, in Manitoba's opinion, had "limits and extent" abundantly sufficient to tax their energies and capabilities and it would be unwise further to increase their responsibilities (154, p. 27). With regard to those parts of the districts of Assiniboia, Saskatchewan, and Athabaska that were not included in the Province of Saskatchewan when it was formed in 1905, Manitoba requested that they be given to her to preserve "geographical" symmetry and because they formed part of the territory in which Manitoba had asked an extension of boundaries for over 25 years. Manitoba also pointed out that, as the area was sparsely populated, the reasons given in 1905 for refusing her the strip of territory in the Province of Saskatchewan immediately to the west of the boundary of Manitoba did not apply. But the strongest argument for Manitoba, in her own view, was that the Legislature of the Northwest Territories, prior to the creation of the Province of Saskatchewan, had stated that it had no pronounced views on the territory north of Lakes Winnipegosis and Manitoba and that it might be given to Manitoba.

THE CLAIMS OF QUEBEC

The claim of the province of Quebec to a northern extension was made in a memorial from its Executive Council, dated November 9, 1907, which requested the Government of Canada to annex to the province all the area between its northern boundary and Hudson Strait and between Hudson Bay, the Atlantic Ocean, and the "skirt of land" along the Atlantic Ocean that was "supposed to belong to Newfoundland", including the islands in Hudson Bay adjacent to the mainland. Specifically mentioned were the Ottawa, Sleepers, Bakers Dozen, Belcher, North Belcher, King George, Mansel, and Charles Islands, the islands of Ungava Bay, and the Button Islands (43, col. 12786).

This claim was supported by a number of arguments. First of all, Quebec maintained that the area requested formed part of the province in a geographical sense, because it was wholly isolated from all other parts of Canada by a wide expanse of sea. Furthermore, it was maintained that this undeveloped region was necessary to Quebec, in order to protect the timber, fish, and game over much of the actual territory of the province, because the natives who occupied Ungava, in coming south to hunt in Quebec, were the cause of forest fires and the destruction of fish and wild life. Having caused this havoc they returned to their own "region", where they were beyond reach of the regulations made by the government of Quebec for the protection of its natural resources.

Quebec also took the view that, because of its geographical position, Ungava had everything to gain in becoming part of the province, as the government of Quebec was the most suitably situated to administer and develop Ungava's natural resources. Ungava offered to the other provinces neither advantage nor interest, and the Dominion Government could not adequately administer the area without special and expensive organization.

Finally, the enlargement of its boundaries was claimed by Quebec as compensation for any advantages that Ontario, Manitoba, and Saskatchewan would gain if they were extended to the western shore of Hudson Bay.

THE DECISIONS

It appears that the Government of Canada gave consideration to the creation of entirely new provinces out of the areas lying north of Manitoba, Ontario, and Quebec but concluded that climatic conditions were such that new provinces could not be created. "If then, that territory cannot be turned into new provinces, does it not seem that the best way to deal with it is to annex it to the existing provinces?" said the Prime Minister (44, col. 4340). Having settled the policy, attention was then given to the details of implementing it. The claims of Saskatchewan were rejected because the weight of argument to have territory lying north of Manitoba and west of Saskatchewan allotted to either province was in favour of Manitoba (43, col. 12779). The government of the day was also prepared to admit the claim of Manitoba to have its boundary extended northward to the 60th parallel, but the boundary on the east presented difficulties because the claims of Ontario and Manitoba overlapped.

Manitoba claimed an extension eastward to include the area between Albany River and Hudson Bay, to a meridian line drawn from the confluence of Mississippi and Ohio Rivers, this eastern meridian being based on Manitoba's earlier claims in 1881. Ontario claimed an extension westward to Churchill River.

The government did not think it advisable to agree to Manitoba's claimed eastward limit, because the boundary would have been brought into the vicinity of the longitude of Fort William, Port Arthur, and Lake Nipigon (43, col. 12779). Neither could it agree to Ontario's claimed western boundary.

The Prime Minister of Canada pointed out that the new railway to Hudson Bay would probably have its terminus at Churchill, as Churchill had the best, and perhaps the only, harbour on Hudson Bay. He then expressed the view that, in these circumstances, a town of some proportions would eventually grow up at the mouth, and on both sides, of Churchill River. If the river formed a provincial boundary then part of the town would be in Ontario and the other part in Manitoba. Then "complications would arise and the progress of the city might be materially retarded for the necessity of having legislation either from one province or the other. Therefore, it is far preferable, far more convenient and far more suitable in every possible way that the city be either in one province or the other" (43, col. 12780).

Ultimately the government decided to fix the northeastern boundary of Manitoba from the then northeast corner of the province over the height of land between Hayes River and Nelson River on one side and that between Hayes and Severn Rivers on the other. However, it was discovered that this definition might lead to complications because the height of land between the Hayes and the Severn did not extend all the way to the shore of Hudson Bay, but was met some distance from the shore by another height of land running east and west. Therefore, in order to follow the principles on which the definition was based and yet avoid a controversial description, the boundary had to be expressed differently, and it was determined that it should be a straight line from the northeast corner of the then boundary of Manitoba to the east end of Island Lake and thence on a straight line to the point where the 89th meridian of west longitude intersects the shore line of Hudson Bay. A resolution recommending this and the above northern and western boundaries was passed by the House of Commons in 1908 (43, col. 12814). No decision was made in 1908 regarding the extension of Quebec, beyond the proposal that, subject to the consent of the Legislature of the Province of Quebec, it would be expedient to extend the boundaries of that province so as to include all the territory to the north of it and extending to the waters of James Bay and Hudson Bay, and the entrance thereto from the sea (43, col. 12814).

Beyond the passing of these resolutions, however, no further action was taken on these extensions until February 1912, when Bills were passed incorporating the proposed extensions, with the exception that Quebec was not enlarged so as to include the coastal islands, as the province had requested. In fact, no coastal islands were included in any of the three provincial extensions. One reason was the difficulty of giving a description of such islands that would be sufficiently definite. Another was that the islands might be necessary for Dominion purposes in connection with navigation and defence (44, col. 5270). The boundary extensions were described as follows:

Ontario

"Commencing at the most northerly point of the western boundary of the province of Ontario as determined by "The Canada (Ontario Boundary) Act, 1889", chapter 28 of the statutes of 1889 of the United Kingdom (the said westerly boundary being the easterly boundary of the province of Manitoba); thence continuing due north along the same meridian to the intersection thereof with the centre of the road allowance on the twelfth base line of the system of Dominion Land Surveys; thence north-easterly in a right line to the most eastern point of Island lake, as shown in approximate latitude 53°30' and longitude 93°40' on the railway map of the Dominion of Canada, published, on the scale of thirty-five miles to one inch, in the year one thousand nine hundred and eight, by the authority of the Minister of the Interior; thence northeasterly in a right line to the point where the eighty-ninth meridian of west longitude intersects the southern shore of Hudson bay; thence easterly and southerly following the shore of the said bay to the point where the northerly boundary of the province of Ontario as established under the said Act intersects the shore of James bay; thence westward along the said boundary as established by the said Act to the place of commencement" (178, pp. 246-7).

Quebec

"Commencing at the point at the mouth of East Main river where it empties into James bay, the said point being the western termination of the northern boundary of the province of Quebec as established by chapter 3 of the statutes of 1898, entitled An Act respecting the north-western, northern and north-eastern boundaries of the province of Quebec; thence northerly and easterly along the shores of Hudson bay and Hudson strait; thence southerly, easterly and northerly along the shore of Ungava bay and the shore of the said strait; thence easterly along the shore of the said strait to the boundary of the territory over which the island of Newfoundland has lawful jurisdiction; thence southeasterly along the westerly boundary of the said last mentioned territory to the middle of the Bay du Rigolet or Hamilton Inlet; thence westerly along the northern boundary of the province of Quebec as established by the said Act to the place of commencement" (179, p. 248).

Manitoba

"Commencing where the sixtieth parallel of north latitude intersects the western shore of Hudson Bay; thence westerly along the said parallel of latitude to the northeast corner of the province of Saskatchewan; thence southerly along the easterly boundary of the province of Saskatchewan to the international boundary dividing Canada from the United States; thence easterly along the said international boundary to the point where the said international boundary turns due north; thence north along the said international boundary to the most northerly point thereof at or near the northwest angle of the Lake of the Woods; thence continuing due north along the westerly boundary of the province of Ontario, by virtue of "The Canada (Ontario Boundary) Act, 1889", chapter 28 of the statutes of 1889 of the United Kingdom, (the said westerly boundary being the easterly boundary of the province of Manitoba) to the most northerly point of the said boundary common to the two provinces under the said Act; thence continuing due north along the same meridian to the intersection thereof with the centre of the road allowance on the twelfth base line of the system of Dominion Land Surveys; thence northeasterly in a right line to the most easterly point of Island Lake, as shown in approximate latitude 53°30′ and longitude 93°40′ on the railway map of the Dominion of Canada published, on the scale of thirty-five miles to one inch, in the year one thousand nine hundred and eight, by the authority of the Minister of the Interior; thence northeasterly in a right line to the point where the eighty-ninth meridian of west longitude intersects the southern shore of Hudson Bay; thence westerly and northerly following the shores of the said Bay to the place of commencement" (177, p. 252).

THE PROVISIONAL DISTRICTS

To bring the Provisional Districts into conformity with the changes in boundaries effected in 1905 and 1912, their boundaries were further defined in 1918 by an Order in Council, which was to take effect in 1920.

Mackenzie was described as the area between the Yukon Territory, the 60th parallel of latitude, the continental shore of the Arctic Ocean, and the 2nd meridian in the Dominion Lands System.

Keewatin's boundaries were as follows:

"Commencing at the point where the second meridian . . . . intersects the continental shore of the Arctic Ocean, thence easterly along the said shore to the most northerly point of Spence Bay, between Franklin Isthmus and Boothia Peninsula; thence northeasterly in a straight line across Boothia Isthmus to the most southwesterly point of Lord Mayor Bay in the Gulf of Boothia; thence southeasterly along the shore of the said Gulf to the most southerly point thereof; thence southerly in a straight line across Rae Isthmus to the most northwesterly point of Repulse Bay; thence southeasterly along the middle of Repulse Bay to Frozen straight; thence southerly along the middle line of Frozen straight to Fox Channel; thence southeasterly in a straight line to the most northerly point of Cape Wolstenholme in the Province of Quebec; thence southerly following the eastern shore of Hudson Bay to James Bay, thence southerly following the eastern shore of James Bay to the point where it is intersected by the boundary between the Provinces of Quebec and Ontario, thence northerly following the western shore of James Bay to Hudson, Bay, thence westerly . . . . and northwesterly following the southern shore of Hudson Bay to the point where it is intersected by the parallel of the sixtieth degree of north latitude, thence westerly along the said parallel to the second meridian . . . . thence northerly along the said meridian to the point of beginning" (26).

Franklin was described as consisting of that part of the Northwest Territories not included in Mackenzie and Keewatin.

It will be noted that Franklin embraced the whole of Hudson Strait and Keewatin the whole of Hudson Bay with a westerly boundary along the 2nd meridian (102 degrees west). The latter boundary was probably chosen as the dividing line between Mackenzie and Keewatin partly for its convenience, as it was merely a continuation of the boundary between Manitoba and Saskatchewan, and partly because it roughly divides those areas of continental Canada north of 60 degrees north that are approached by the Hudson Bay-Hudson Strait route from those approached via Mackenzie River and its tributaries. In this sense, therefore, that part of the 2nd meridian north of the 60th parallel may in 1918 have been considered as an approximation to a watershed boundary. However, subsequent knowledge of the general area through which it passes has shown that such approximation is not very close.

These inter-territorial boundaries were established before there were any settlements in the boundary areas. Where settlements have subsequently been set up, some rather odd situations have developed. For example, the settlement of Spence Bay on Boothia Isthmus, 100 miles removed from its nearest neighbour, consists of two small groups of buildings, with a total white population of five. One group forms the Hudson's Bay Company post, and the other the R.C.M.P. post. Yet the boundary as delimited in 1918 places the former in the District of Franklin and the latter in the District of Keewatin. However, the nature of the inter-territorial boundaries is such that, in present circumstances, such a situation is of academic interest only.

With the passage of the Order in Council of 1918, the political map of Canada as it existed prior to the Privy Council decision on the Newfoundland-Labrador boundary, came into being (*See* Figure 10). In the main, however, only the development of the major political boundaries from the point of view of delimitation has been dealt with. A boundary can hardly be described as "fixed" until it has been demarcated in some way or other.

CHAPTER VIII

BOUNDARY DEMARCATION AND ADMINISTRATION

The place of boundary demarcation in the general process of boundary evolution has already been described in the introduction to this work. It means the marking of a boundary by some physical means. Boundary delimitation, as the foregoing chapters have shown, is a matter that may be decided upon quite rapidly or may occur after years of deliberation and negotiation, but the marking of a boundary upon the surface of the earth involves different problems.

THE PROCESS OF BOUNDARY DEMARCATION

The change from delimitation to demarcation is no easy one. It is easiest if the delimitation has been stated in such a manner that demarcation can begin as merely a matter of routine surveying. Such delimitation, however, has not always occurred in Canada.

Faulty delimitations have been attributed to inexact definition, unsuitable definition, contradictory definition, and unascertainable previous jurisdiction (69, p. 417). It has been shown that the earliest boundary delimitations in the northern part of North America were often arbitrary in their essential character and were usually vaguely worded and phrased, often having been drawn up by authorities far removed from the area involved. Even if the scene had been visited, detailed knowledge of it was usually scanty, and maps quite inadequate. In fact many of the early documents expressly included the right, if not the obligation, to explore a loosely defined area.

The development from delimitation to demarcation is particularly difficult, however, if a boundary is defined by natural features of the landscape, unless the definition includes a detailed account of the course of the boundary in relation to such features. Yet it was precisely these outstanding physical features that were seized upon in the relatively unknown parts of Canada in order to provide what were considered to be indisputable points of reference in boundary documents. The northern part of the Ontario-Quebec boundary was supposed to be the due north line from the "head" of Lake Timiskaming, but in 1872-73 the surveyors of the southern end of this line found no definite feature that they could agree upon as the "head" of the lake. They found two rivers flowing into the lake from the north, the two mouths being each broken up into five channels by four islands, with the two outside channels about 2½ miles apart in longitude (91, p. 143). As a result, a decision acceptable to both governments had to be made.

The almost endless negotiations regarding the northern and western boundaries of New Brunswick resulted from another instance of faulty delimitation based on topographic features. In fact the only two inter-provincial boundaries still unsettled are of this nature—the Quebec-Newfoundland boundary and the Quebec-Ontario boundary between the 45th parallel and Lake St. Francis. The first of these boundaries is supposed to follow a watershed for the most part, but the location of the watershed is very difficult to establish on the ground. When it is recalled that the watershed between British Columbia and Alberta, long considered one of the most sharply defined in the world, was described by the surveyors as being "by no means so well defined on the ground as might be supposed" (135, I, p. 2), the nature of the problem in Quebec-Newfoundland may be better appreciated.

Even when boundaries are delimited in terms of latitude and longitude, demarcation is not always a simple matter. The Canada-Alaska boundary along the 141st Meridian was completely defined, but the requirements for its demarcation could not be completely carried out owing to the physical nature of the terrain (84, p. 58).

However, as interest in the New World developed, and as its potential value came to be appreciated, more precise delimitation, and ultimately demarcation, became necessary. Parallel with these developments came closer and more effective administration, as well as new techniques in surveying and mapping, which made the task of demarcation much easier. Demarcation thus came to be regarded as an essential part of all boundary problems.

But because of the way in which it has evolved, boundary demarcation, especially in Canada, is not even merely a matter of surveying and monumenting, for its ultimate objective must be the establishment of a true and unalterable boundary according to law, so that no possible dispute in regard to its position can arise in the future. It involves the following steps[1]:

(a) The determination of the boundary line from documents of delimitation and field surveys.
(b) The marking of the boundary line on the ground, which involves the selection of sites for, as well as the erection of, monuments and markers.
(c) Plotting the location of the markers on large-scale maps.
(d) Drawing the boundary line on the map in accordance with the treaty of delimitation.
(e) Describing completely the boundary area from marker to marker, as well as the markers themselves.
(f) Preparing a comprehensive report for transmission to the governments concerned.

THE DEVELOPMENT OF BOUNDARY DEMARCATION IN CANADA

NATIONAL NECESSITY

When the United States of America became independent and the boundary between it and territory remaining British was decided upon, it passed through some relatively thickly populated areas, and demarcation of the "dividing line", therefore, became an immediate necessity.

The present boundary between Quebec and New York and Vermont had been demarcated in 1771-74 as a boundary between British provinces. But the work was carried out in a rather crude manner, and accurate demarcation really dates from 1783.

The delimitations included in the treaty of peace with the United States were, however, the subject of much dispute, as has already been pointed out, and the first monument under its provisions for demarcation was not erected until 1797, at the source of the "true River St. Croix".

The Treaty of Ghent, 1814, provided for two commissioners to ascertain the position of the boundary, as delimited in the treaty, from the source of St. Croix River to the St. Lawrence. Their "exploring line" between the source of St. Croix River and St. John River was marked and surveyed in 1817 and 1818 (See Plate III B). This work also included the erection of a monument on the south bank of the St. Lawrence to mark the western end of the 45th parallel section of the boundary. The commissioners, however, did not agree on the interpretation of the whole of the St. Croix-St. Lawrence boundary as delimited in the treaty, and no decision was reached until 1842, when the so-called "Webster-Ashburton" Treaty was negotiated.

[1]Many more details are included in *Instructions to Demarcation Commissions pursuant to the Paris Treaties* (84, pp. 229-239).

This treaty not only delimited the boundary more precisely but also provided for surveying and marking it. This was carried out from 1843 to 1845. The section of this boundary between the source of St. Croix River and St. John River ("The North Line") followed the "exploring line" of 1817-18 and the 45th parallel ("The West Line") section followed the line surveyed in 1771-74. The resurvey of the latter disclosed that it diverged greatly, though not consistently, from the line it was supposed to follow (76, p. 332), but it was nevertheless accepted as the "true boundary".

The Treaty of Ghent, 1814, also provided for the fixing and determining of the part of the International Boundary from the most northwesterly point of Lake of the Woods to Lake Superior and empowered the commissioners to cause to be surveyed and marked such parts as required it. Comparatively little was known about the area involved, as the Mitchell map of 1755 indicated, and the survey made under the Treaty of Ghent was the first systematic one made in the area. It was carried out in 1824, and several places on the boundary were marked by means of monuments (77, pp. 217-218).

The next part of the International Boundary to be determined and marked on the ground was the section west of the summit of the Rocky Mountains. This was carried out in 1857-61. At that time, however, the country adjacent to the boundary was sparsely inhabited and, in the high mountainous sections, settlement appeared unlikely at least for some time to come. Therefore, the boundary was demarcated through settled regions and at prominent stream crossings only, the intervals between marked sections being, in some cases, as much as 25 miles (79, p. XIV).

The "plains section" of the 49th Parallel between the Rockies and Lake of the Woods was first surveyed and marked in 1872-75. The open character of the country rendered operations comparatively simple, and the line was marked at frequent intervals. But as transportation facilities were developed, and as the country on each side of the boundary became more populated, it became clear that this section of the boundary demanded a more definite demarcation, particularly at points where there were trails, or where grass and water were found in more than usual abundance and so caused cattle to cross into Canada from the United States. The R.C.M.P. were responsible for carrying out the quarantine regulations and were, at times, kept in the saddle almost day and night driving American cattle back across the border. Occasionally these cattle were seized under Canadian customs regulations, but the authorities were handicapped by not being able to locate the boundary for miles at a stretch. Some of these difficulties arose from the fact that many of the original monuments in this section had been merely mounds of earth, which had deteriorated greatly since their construction (*See* Plate I).

In 1898, questions as to the adequacy of the demarcation of the 49th Parallel west of the Rockies began to arise, and in 1899 similar problems arose regarding the Quebec-New York line. The boundaries through the water channels to the Atlantic and Pacific Oceans also remained to be marked, although general maps of the boundaries in these areas had been prepared, and some range marks had been erected on the Atlantic part as early as 1893, following the seizure by Canada of seven American fishing vessels on the ground that they were operating in Canadian waters.

Finally, in 1908, a treaty was adopted by Canada and the United States of America providing for a more complete demarcation of the land and water parts of the whole International Boundary. It described the boundary in eight sections and provided for the appointment of a joint commission to locate or restore previously established marks and to place new marks in unmarked sections. The boundary through the St. Lawrence River and the Great Lakes was assigned to the International Waterways Commission, and the remainder of the boundary to the International Boundary Commission. The work under the treaty of 1908 was completed in the 1930s.

The treaty of 1908, however, did not include the boundary between Canada and Alaska. This boundary was surveyed and demarcated from 1904 to 1913, following an international convention signed in 1906 (74, p. 15; 80, p. xiii).

PROVINCIAL EXPEDIENCY

Unlike Canada's international boundaries, at least those with the United States, her interprovincial boundaries were not demarcated until it became expedient to do so. This did not take place until settlement occurred or was immediately anticipated in the boundary region, or until some administrative problem, usually connected with natural resources, arose. The only exception was the Quebec-New Brunswick boundary, which was demarcated in 1853-55 (*See* Plate V B). This was the first of Canada's interprovincial boundaries to be demarcated and it did not run through a densely populated area. But since its establishment depended on the settlement of the Quebec-United States boundary, this demarcation can be said to be more closely tied to international necessity than to provincial expediency.

The New Brunswick-Nova Scotia boundary was not demarcated until 1859, although the main course of the boundary became recognized by the people who lived near it by about 1800. The delay was partly due to the difficulty of demarcation at the source of the River Misseguash. It rises in an area of floating bogs, and the numerous small streams and lakes in the vicinity made it difficult to determine the true source of the river, and its various windings in the upper reaches. Ultimately the boundary did not attempt to follow these windings, but followed compass lines along the general direction of the river (52, pp. 368-69). Apart from this, the only other interprovincial boundary that ran through settled country before 1867 was the southern part of the Quebec-Ontario boundary. As this happened to be mainly the Ottawa River, demarcation was unnecessary until settlement spread north of Lake Timiskaming. This began in 1872-74 when the "due north line" from Lake Timiskaming was surveyed to the height of land between Hudson Bay drainage and Great Lakes drainage, some 42 miles north of the zero point on the lake (92, p. 144).

Not until 1897 did further interprovincial demarcation occur. It was pointed out by the Dominion Government in 1887 that "for judical and other purposes it is very important that the portion of the Ontario-Manitoba boundary extending from the Northwest angle of Lake of the Woods to Winnipeg river be defined at once". This was not done, however, until 1897, by which time the necessity had become even more urgent (136, p. 6) (*See* Plate V A).

Hardly had this survey been completed than the next began, but this time in a more remote area—northwestern British Columbia. For in 1898, owing to the discovery of gold in the Klondike and the consequent influx of people to the area, questions of jurisdiction arose between the British Columbia and Dominion Governments. Following representations by British Columbia, the Minister of the Interior directed that the boundary between British Columbia and the newly formed Yukon Territory be demarcated. This work was carried on during the years 1899-1901 and again in 1907-1908. About 157 miles of boundary were surveyed and marked on the ground. Commencing on the west side of Teslin Lake, the line runs westward to Tatshenshini River, with a break of 9 miles in the mountainous country between Takhini and Hudson Rivers. It was not considered necessary to survey the 65 miles of permanently snow-covered mountains from Tatshenshini River westward to the Alaska border (24, p. 136).

In the meantime, the southeastern part of British Columbia was being developed. Valuable coal deposits had been located at widely separated points in the region of the boundary, which was to follow the watershed of the Rocky Mountains. As a result, leases of coal lands had been issued by both the Dominion and the province. In some instances the descriptions of these leases were based on surveys that assumed a provisional boundary, as the watershed was very ill-defined in places. As a result, surveys made by Dominion and Provincial surveyors were based on differing provisional boundaries, and often overlapped. This in turn led to problems of administration, such as the collection of royalties on coal and the control of mining operations under the respective statutes of the Dominion or the province.

Administration of the extensive forest resources on either side of the watershed also stressed the necessity for demarcating the boundary so that surveyors in private practice, timber lessees, fire wardens, and game guardians could govern their activities accordingly (135, I, p. 2).

In 1913, instructions were issued for the demarcation of the boundary between British Columbia and Alberta between the International Boundary and the 120th degree of longitude, and the work was completed by 1916. The instructions issued were very full, and one paragraph is particularly enlightening, for it stated that the parts of the boundary that required first attention were the Crowsnest Pass, owing to the proximity of mining properties; the Vermilion Pass, owing to the construction of the motor road from Banff to Windermere; the Howse Pass, owing to the proximity of timber claims; the Kicking Horse Pass, Simpson Pass, and White Man Pass, owing to their lying within or adjacent to populated areas; the Athabasca Pass, which was a possible railway route; the South Kootenay, the North Kootenay, North Fork, and Kananaskis Passes; the Moose Pass, which had some importance as a possible route to the north via Smoky River, and the Robson Pass, "which is of no importance, except as one of the most striking scenic centres of the entire mountain region" (135, p. 8).

Settlement east of the Rockies, however, was also spreading northwards, and with it the need for the accurate location of provincial boundaries. In 1906, owing to the activity of prospectors, lumbermen, clay-belt investigators, and trans-continental railway builders in what was then northern Ontario and Quebec, the interprovincial boundary was demarcated for a further 47 miles northward to Okikodisek River, a point in the neighbourhood of the proposed Grand Trunk Pacific Railway. In the following year the boundary was further demarcated for an additional 51 miles (91, p. 144).

Presumably for somewhat similar reasons, accentuated by the boundary extensions of 1912, the necessity for further demarcating the boundary between Ontario and Manitoba was discussed by the governments of those provinces and the Dominion during 1913 and 1914, but owing to the outbreak of World War I the matter was left in abeyance until 1920. In that year the Dominion Land Surveyor who had been surveying mineral claims in the Rice Lake district for several years reported that claims were being staked near the interprovincial boundary, and called attention to the necessity for an early demarcation of the line from Winnipeg River northerly through the mining district. It was realized that the question had now reached a stage where further delay would probably be followed by serious complications, and the work proceeded in 1921 and 1922 (136, p. 8); the meridian section of the boundary was completed to the 12th Base Line of the Dominion Lands System.

The northward course of settlement had by this time extended well into the Peace River area of northern Alberta and British Columbia. Bisected as this area was by the meridional boundary between these two provinces, which had never been demarcated, jurisdictional overlapping again occurred, as it had earlier in the watershed section of this interprovincial boundary.

As had occurred before 1913, a provisional boundary line had been run by the government of British Columbia, which did not coincide with the surveys made in the area by the Dominion Government. It was also necessary to survey and demarcate the 120th meridian south to its intersection with the "summit of the Rocky Mountains" so as to determine the point at which the interprovincial boundary ceased to follow the "summit". "Finally it was desired to establish the boundary across Peace River—that most noble artery of Northland traffic —and the unsurveyed country to the north of it, with a view to the proper administration by the adjoining Provinces of their respective laws" (135, p. 85).

The survey of the 120th meridian was carried out from 1922-24, and at the end of their operations the surveyors had reached almost to latitude $57\frac{1}{2}$ degrees north. At this point it was decided to discontinue the survey for the time being as the remaining 174 miles still to be surveyed ran through uninhabited and unproductive country.

The years 1929 and 1930 saw the further demarcation of the Manitoba-Ontario boundary from the 12th Base Line of the Dominion Lands System to Island Lake, and in 1930-31 the remainder of the northern boundary between Quebec and Ontario was demarcated. This became necessary owing to the still further extension northward of the activities of trappers, lumbermen, prospectors, and railway builders, and resulted in the first demarcated inter-provincial boundary to reach Canada's northern coasts, at James Bay.

In 1937, the survey of the Ontario-Manitoba boundary was extended to Echoing River, and the following year active development of the mining and fur industries made it appear necessary for administrative purposes to complete the demarcation of that part of the 110th meridian of longitude (the 4th meridian of the Dominion Lands System) that formed an interprovincial boundary. It has already been pointed out that this boundary was not delimited as an inter-provincial boundary until 1905, but by 1912 it had been completely demarcated from the International Boundary to the south shore of Lake Athabasca. The great difficulties of measuring a line across so large a body of water made it seem inadvisable to produce it farther at that time (192, p. 75).

World War II brought great activity to the Canadian northwest. Among these activities was the construction of the Alaska Military Highway from Dawson Creek, B.C., to Fairbanks, Alaska, in 1942 and 1943. It was known that this highway crossed the northern boundary of British Columbia at several points, but the exact location of the crossings was not known as the boundary had never been surveyed. The matter was brought to the attention of the governments concerned, with the result that Orders in Council were passed by both, stating that "the resulting activity, in the vicinity of the boundary area, makes it necessary that the boundary line be surveyed and marked on the ground for administrative purposes" (24, p. 137).

The work was commenced in 1945 on the west side of Teslin Lake, at a boundary monument established in the survey of 1899, and had been extended eastward to almost 127°30'W. by 1948, those parts of the boundary known to be nearest the highway having been demarcated first.

The boundary that has been most recently demarcated is the remaining section of the Ontario-Manitoba boundary between Echoing River and Hudson Bay. Its terminal point, where the 89th meridian of longitude intersects the shore of Hudson Bay, was reached during 1948. Even more recently, the discovery of minerals in the northern part of the province of Alberta has led to the beginning of the demarcation of the northern boundary of the province—the 60th parallel of latitude. The demand for mining and oil leases called for precise survey and "accurate ground markings" and the work was begun in January 1951.

98

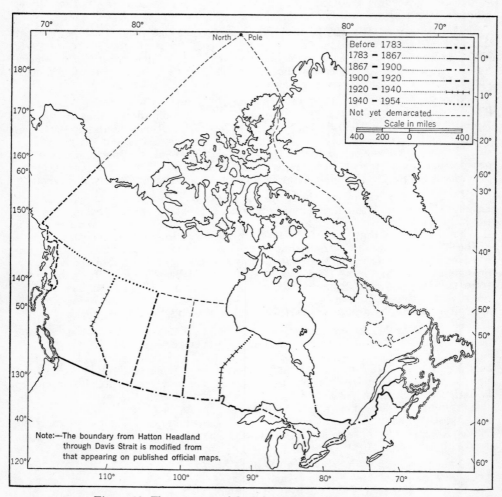

Figure 21. The progress of boundary demarcation in Canada.

Thus the interprovincial boundaries have to a very large extent been demarcated. Where demarcation has not yet occurred, the provinces have, generally speaking, found it inexpedient to do so. In 1950, the Controller of Surveys for the province of Saskatchewan said:

"The north half of the Manitoba-Saskatchewan boundary is not yet surveyed. Probably there will not be a need for same until mineral development and increased population in the vicinity of the boundary warrant delineation of the provinces eastern limit. The survey of the northern boundary of the province has not yet been made and, here again, the necessity of same will depend upon mineral development".

Yet, by 1953, uranium had been discovered at Martin Lake, only 25 miles south of the northern boundary of Saskatchewan. Since "further discoveries and stakings could spill over into the Territories, it has become necessary to survey a portion of the boundary. To do so will also delineate the respective interests of the province and the Northwest Territories in regard to administration and management of fish, game and hydro-electric resources" (148a, p. 169). A Saskatchewan-Northwest Territories Boundary Commission was, therefore, established in that year, for this purpose.

The longest interprovincial boundary that remains to be demarcated is that between Quebec and Newfoundland. This is mainly because the delimitation was a matter of doubt until the comparatively recent decision of the Imperial Privy Council in 1927. Even the initial point of the land boundary between the two provinces at Ance Sablon has never been marked. However, the development of the iron-ore deposits that are intersected by this boundary will undoubtedly call for some demarcation before many years have passed.

For the sake of completeness it should also be mentioned that the boundaries between the territories are not demarcated. The main reason is that demarcation is unnecessary, as territorial boundaries do not separate areas that have different basic administrations. They are all under the control of Ottawa, and any revenue derived from them accrues to the Federal Government. For similar reasons, so long as the three "Prairie Provinces" did not have control of their natural resources they were not anxious to bear the expense of boundary demarcation (136, p. 5).

METHODS OF BOUNDARY DEMARCATION

Boundaries today are usually marked by the erection of stones, signs, beacons, pillars, or monuments, particularly if they do not follow prominent natural features.

MONUMENTS

The type of marker used in Canada has varied considerably. Generally, because of the great distances involved, as well as the fact that demarcation has often taken place in remote regions where transportation is a limiting factor, boundary pillars have been built of whatever materials could be found at hand. For these reasons the earliest boundary monuments were frequently of very simple construction, although if, as time went on, the adjacent areas became settled, the early rudimentary markers were replaced by more permanent ones (*See* Plate III B).

The 1771-74 survey of the 45th parallel was merely a compass line marked by blazes on trees. When re-examined in 1843, these marks were still visible, but iron monuments were erected along the line at every point of deflexion (76, p. 310).

David Thompson, who first surveyed and demarcated the part of the boundary between Lake of the Woods and Lake Superior:

"having arrived at the 49th degree of north latitude . . . there placed a heap of large stones with several pickets well driven into the ground, at the first angle of this Lake there being no stones within several miles we erected a square monument of Logs of 12 feet high by 7 feet width, the lower part of Oak, the upper part of Aspin—and nailed to it a Tin Plate marked the North West Corner of the Lake of the Woods No. 1—proceeding northward at the second Angle of the Lake we erected a Pyramid of stones 7 feet high by 4 feet square at the Base and a Cedar post in its centre nailed a Tin Plate pierced" (77, p. 218).

The interprovincial demarcation shows the same variety in types of monuments. The original demarcation of the boundary between New Brunswick and Nova Scotia was partly carried out by placing hackmatack (larch) posts one-fourth of a mile apart along the line. On the Alberta-Saskatchewan boundary, some monuments were merely mounds of sand, no stone being available (147). On the northern part of the Ontario-Quebec boundary, aluminium plaques were nailed to blazed trees (91, p. 150).

In recent times, it has become a common practice to mark parts, at least, of the interprovincial boundaries by means of short metal posts, which are planted in the ground, and mounds and trenches or stone mounds, which are used as markers (Plate II B).

Unless the boundary is clearly marked by a pronounced physical feature, or is in uninhabited or inaccessible country, it is usual to endeavour to make the monuments intervisible. This has usually been interpreted to mean, in Canada, that each monument should be visible from one or more other monuments, though not necessarily from the nearest (74, p. 187).

Each monument erected along a Canadian boundary is also numbered, usually consecutively from one end of the line, and fully described. The description includes all data that might help to relocate the monument if misplaced, destroyed, or obscured.

THE BOUNDARY VISTA

Where a boundary crosses wooded land, a path or "vista" is normally cut on each side of the line. The width of the vista varies. Along the Canada-United States boundary it is usually sufficient to produce a 20-foot skyline. Along the interprovincial boundaries a 6-foot skyline is the general rule. The width of clearance necessary on the ground to produce a specified width of vista varies. Along the 120th meridian boundary between Alberta and British Columbia the surface clearance necessary for a 6-foot skyline was 10 to 16 feet according to the nature of the timber (135, I, p. 13).

In some places, as on the meridian section of the Alberta-British Columbia boundary, ground is cleared for some distance around each monument, partly to make the monument conspicuous, but mainly to protect it from forest fire (135, III, p. 94) (See Plate II A).

WATER BOUNDARIES

In the case of water boundaries it is not ordinarily possible to erect monuments along them. But it is possible in certain cases to demarcate such boundaries by using alinements made on markers placed on the banks or with the help of floating buoys or fixed beacons.

The International Boundary between Canadian and United States territorial waters has been demarcated in this manner. By the treaty of 1908, the International Boundary Commissioners required these parts of the boundary to be marked by permanent range marks established on land. The two main water boundaries in question were that through Passamaquoddy Bay to the Atlantic Ocean[1] and that through Georgia, Haro, and Juan de Fuca Straits to the Pacific Ocean. Within the bays and straits the reference points were marked by large, triangular, concrete pyramids, which serve as range marks or cross-range marks for the courses of the boundary (See Plate III A). The boundary farther from the shore is referenced to these existing monuments and lighthouses. Some of the lighthouses used as reference marks are frame structures. In order to provide for the recovery of their accurate location should they be destroyed or replaced, concrete witness marks of various designs have been erected, their distances and directions from the lighthouses being accurately determined (75, pp. 57, 58).

The boundary through the Great Lakes and other waterways between the point of intersection of the 45th parallel and the St. Lawrence River and the mouth of Pigeon River is similarly marked in accordance with the following terms of the Treaty of 1908 (75, p. 16):

". . . the said Commissioners shall so far as practicable mark the course of this entire boundary . . . by buoys and monuments in the waterways and by permanent range marks established on the adjacent shores or islands, and by such other boundary marks and at such points as in the judgment of the Commissioners it is desirable that the boundary should be so marked".

With regard to the national boundaries, between the territorial waters of Canada and the high seas, an Order in Council in 1937 not only defined certain of the limits of Canadian territorial waters, but also directed that these limits be mapped. Although it would be almost impracticable to demarcate these boundaries completely, some of the means of demarcation described above might have been used following this Order in Council, but were not. No Canadian territorial waters, therefore, have yet been demarcated, although marking their limits on accurate maps is a step in this direction.

MAINTENANCE AND ADMINISTRATION

A demarcated boundary is a man-made structure, and, like other man-made structures, requires maintenance. Without maintenance a demarcated boundary will deteriorate and perhaps disappear.

In Canada, monuments suffer deterioration from frost. Freezing in cracks may destroy concrete and stone markers and freezing of the soil often tilts the monument. In some instances monuments have been destroyed or moved by human agencies. For example, 4 years after the survey of the Vermont-Quebec boundary under the Treaty of 1842, the complaints that Monument 560 in the village of Beebe Plain had been moved from its original position were found to be justified.

The greatest maintenance problems in Canada, however, are concerned with the boundary vistas. These fill in with new growth almost as soon as they are cut and need to be cleared periodically. Such problems were exemplified during the retracement of part of the northern boundary between Quebec and Ontario, for in places the line was so completely overgrown that it could not be recognized by the surveyors even when they knew they were actually on it. This was true not only of the 58-year old line but of the 26-year old one as well. Some of the monuments were destroyed and some others were so completely covered that they were located only as a result of the surveyors' measurements (91, p. 145).

---

[1] The final extension of this boundary to the high seas was not adopted until the Boundary Treaty of 1925.

88589—8

To deal with these problems on long or important boundaries a permanent maintenance body was needed. For example, after 1915 it became apparent that on the section of the Canada-United States boundary through the St. Lawrence River, the Great Lakes, and their connecting waterways, several monuments required moving or repairing. Furthermore, on bridges being built across the connecting waterways, the boundary crossings were not marked, and a new growth of timber had filled in a great deal of the boundary vista. This need for maintaining an effective boundary led to the negotiation of a special treaty in 1925. Under this treaty, boundary commissioners were empowered to

"inspect the various sections of the boundary line between the United States and the Dominion of Canada and between Alaska and the Dominion of Canada at such times as they shall deem necessary; to repair all damaged monuments and buoys; to relocate and rebuild monuments which have been destroyed; to keep the boundary vistas open, to move boundary monuments to new sites and establish such additional monuments and buoys as they shall deem desirable; to maintain at all times an effective boundary line between the United States and the Dominion of Canada and between Alaska and the Dominion of Canada, as defined by the present treaty and treaties heretofore concluded, or hereafter to be concluded; and to determine the location of any point of the boundary line which may become necessary in the settlement of any question that may arise between the two governments" (190, p. 449).

The commissioners and their staffs are known as the International Boundary Commission. The Commission is divided into two sections, one for Canada and one for the United States.

The Commissioners are required by the treaty of 1925 to submit a joint report to their respective governments at least once in every calendar year. This report must include:

"a statement of inspections made, the monuments and buoys repaired, relocated, rebuilt, moved and established . . . plats and tables certified and signed by the commissioners, giving the locations and geodetic positions of all monuments moved and all additional monuments established within the year, and such other information as may be necessary to keep the boundary maps and records accurately revised" (190, p. 449).

The interprovincial boundaries are not maintained and administered in the same manner because they are relatively less important. As problems arise the provinces involved take the necessary action, which as a rule results in a resurvey of the boundary concerned by a properly constituted Boundary Commission. In the case of the British Columbia-Alberta boundary the report of the Commissioners appointed to demarcate the boundary between the two provinces also stated that:

"In order to deal with all questions in connection with replacing of all monuments which may be destroyed or disturbed, the re-adjustment of any portions of the Boundary and the dealing with any matters concerning the Boundary, it is recommended that the Surveyor General of Canada, the Director of Surveys of Alberta and the Surveyor General of British Columbia be constituted a standing Committee to which all such matters may be referred" (135, III, p. 91).

THE COST OF DEMARCATION AND BOUNDARY ADMINISTRATION

The cost of boundary demarcation and maintenance is no small item in a country such as Canada, where such great distances are involved and where boundaries often traverse terrain that is difficult of access. Boundary demarcation not only involves surveying and monumenting, but also the mapping of the boundary areas. In the case of international boundaries particularly, the surveys have to be accompanied by accurate maps of high quality, which, consequently, involve special expenditures. The cost of producing the charts alone for the International Boundary through the St. Lawrence River and the Great Lakes was estimated at $60,000 in 1908.

Similarly, the cost of monuments alone is by no means inconsiderable. The placing of buoys, monuments, and range marks to mark the Great Lakes-St. Lawrence water boundary in 1908 was estimated to cost $100,000 (81, p. 27). When the British Columbia-Alberta boundary was monumented in 1913-16 each monument was estimated to cost approximately $35 (135, I, p. 23), and along the 120th meridian section of this boundary there are 232 monuments. In more modern times, aircraft have been used to an increasing extent in the surveying and demarcating of boundaries. This was the case with the 168-mile stretch of the Manitoba-Ontario boundary between Echoing River and Hudson Bay, and the total cost of the flying alone was $16,775 (3, p. 139).

In the case of the provincial boundaries, the Federal Government is usually involved in the original survey and demarcation and shares the costs with the provinces in varying proportion, but usually equally, so that each government contributes one-third of the total cost. Maintenance costs are usually divided equally between the two provinces concerned. In the case of the International Boundary Commission, the salaries of each Commissioner and his staff and office expenses are paid by the government concerned, but boundary mainten-ance and other "visible" expenses are shared equally. When it is considered that Canada's International Boundaries are marked by 5,463 monuments, a 20-foot vista through 1,353 miles of wooded areas, and an additional 2,522 reference monuments along the water sections, it will be realized that the cost of maintenance is fairly heavy (3). Some of Canada's expenses in this connec-tion during the last few years are set out in Table II. Occasionally, too, the cost of boundary demarcation has included human lives and suffering as a result of serious accidents to the ground survey personnel. This is particularly true of mountainous country. In 1909, while working on the Canada-Alaska boundary survey, one member of the party broke through the snow cornice of a mountain and fell 2,000 feet to the glacier below, and in 1913 a landslide buried two men at their camp at Cape Muzon in the same boundary area (80, p. 32).

The value of adequate boundary demarcation is almost impossible to express in dollars and cents. During the course of demarcation and maintenance operations in Canada, much exploration and map making has been carried out,

TABLE II

International Boundary Commission (Canadian Section) Expenditures 1945-1955

Fiscal year	Expenditure
1945-46	$32,886
1946-47	$36,348
1947-48	$35,836
1948-49	$44,427
1949-50	$29,177
1950-51	$43,980
1951-52	$51,086
1952-53	$61,122
1953-54	$65,870[1]
1954-55	$69,481[1]

[1] From estimates for the Fiscal Year ending March 31, 1954. Preceding figures from Public Accounts of Canada for the years concerned.

often in areas that before the boundary work were completely unknown. The foregoing pages are full of the difficulties encountered because accurate surveys of boundary areas were lacking. This often resulted in the language of documents relating to boundaries not being sufficiently clear and, therefore, in lengthy and costly litigation over their correct interpretation. The amounts expended by the province of Ontario alone on the settlement of the northerly and westerly boundaries of the province and the arbitration in reference thereto totalled over $15,000 between 1867 and 1879 (88, p. 480), and this was not an international problem. When one thinks of the errors on the Mitchell map and Vancouver's chart the expense of boundary demarcation and maintenance seems a small price to pay for well-defined boundaries.

CHAPTER IX

BOUNDARY ADJUSTMENT AND ADJUSTMENT TO BOUNDARIES

The preceding chapter was concerned with the process and costs of boundary demarcation and administration, and it makes it clear that this phase of boundary evolution may be very costly and time-consuming.

The earlier chapters of this work showed how boundary delimitation occurred in former times. Each step in the evolution of territorial limits was eventually accompanied by a legal document of some kind, and as Canada emerged as a Federal state of ten provinces and two territories, as the need for demarcation grew, and as constitutional processes became more complex, so the legal-geographical ramifications of problems associated with boundaries multiplied.

THE CONSTITUTIONAL PROCESSES OF BOUNDARY CHANGE AND ADJUSTMENT

These aspects of boundaries involve the processes through which adjustments and compromises are arrived at before a final boundary is agreed upon, as well as those that are followed if change or adjustment is needed after the recognized legal establishment of a boundary.

INTERNATIONAL BOUNDARIES

It is a well-known fact, fully substantiated by what has been presented previously, that boundaries between countries are established by treaties made by the sovereign powers concerned. Such boundaries are also adjusted or changed in a similar way. Between 1782 and 1925, the Canada-United States boundary was a subject of negotiation in at least seventeen treaties, conventions, and protocols that have gone into force, as well as others that were not ratified or completed. There have been two arbitrations, and a number of international commissions have been appointed to settle details in dispute relating to the interpretation of treaty provisions (10, p. 33). As Canada's international boundaries are also coincident with provincial boundaries, except where they pass through navigable waters and also with the exception of the Yukon-Alaska boundary, any future change in these international boundaries would appear to require at least legal recognition by the province concerned, as was the case with the change in the International Boundary in the Lake of the Woods area in 1925. By this change, agreed to by Great Britain (on behalf of Canada) and the United States, Manitoba's boundaries also became altered and the change was legally recognized by that province (183) as well as by the Canadian Parliament (180).

INTERPROVINCIAL BOUNDARIES

New provinces may be created by the Government of Canada under the terms of Imperial Acts 34-35, Vict., Ch. 28 (The British North America Act, 1871), which state that

"The Parliament of Canada may from time to time establish new Provinces in any territories forming for the time being part of the Dominion of Canada, but not included in any Province thereof, and may at the time of such establishment, make provision for the constitution and administration of any such Province . . .".

The creation of new provinces out of territories appears to be solely the responsibility of the Federal Parliament, but when once a province has been created, its boundaries cannot be changed by the Federal Parliament without the consent of the province concerned, for the 1871 act states that

"The Parliament of Canada may from time to time, with the consent of the Legislature of any Province of the said Dominion, increase, diminish, or otherwise alter the limits of such Province . . .".

Thus a boundary between two provinces of Canada may be changed only by agreement of the legislatures concerned and the Parliament of Canada. In the case of the Ontario-Manitoba dispute, the Judicial Committee of the Privy Council reported that legislation by the province of Ontario as well as by Canada and the province of Manitoba was necessary to give binding effect to the award of August 3, 1878, and as no such legislation had taken place, said award was not binding.

Even after a boundary has been delimited in an official document and agreed to by all parties concerned, further legal action is necessary after the boundary has been demarcated. Thus, after most of the Alberta-British Columbia boundary had been demarcated, both Provincial Governments (164, 166) as well as the Federal Government (181) passed acts recognizing the boundary as demarcated as the true boundary, whether or not it increased, diminished, or otherwise altered the territory of the respective provinces (*See also* 45b, pp. 1935, 1936).

TERRITORIAL BOUNDARIES

A boundary between a province and a territory is fixed by joint action of the Federal Parliament and the legislature of the province concerned.

Boundaries between territories are fixed by federal action alone, by an Act of Parliament. So far there has only been one instance of this, namely the Yukon-Northwest Territories boundary.

Boundaries within territories, e.g., district boundaries, are also determined solely by Federal authorities, either by an Order in Council or an Act of Parliament. It would appear from Orders in Council of 1882, 1895, 1897, and 1918 that an Order in Council is all that is needed for the creation and delimitation of territorial districts. However, legislation was resorted to in 1906 to define the boundaries of Mackenzie, Yukon, Keewatin, and Ungava in their entirety, and Keewatin, the first district to be created, was the result of an Act of Parliament as early as 1876.

Disputes between provinces regarding boundaries, unless started before December 1958, are now settled by the Supreme Court of Canada, whose decisions are final. Until 1948, the final Court of Appeal was the Imperial Privy Council, by Imperial Act, 3-4 Wm. IV, Cap. 41.

The above summary re-emphasizes that not only has it cost a great deal to establish the present boundaries of Canada, both with regard to delimitation and demarcation, but it may also be a costly and lengthy process to adjust or change an established boundary. Nevertheless, there have been many advocates of changes since 1912.

REVIEW OF SUGGESTIONS CONCERNING BOUNDARY CHANGES

NORTHERN ONTARIO

The recognition that northern Ontario is regionally different from the rest of the province and that it, therefore, has problems that are peculiar to it has manifested itself in many different ways. The Northern Ontario Citizens Planning Conference, for example, passed a resolution in 1950 to the effect that steps be immediately taken to set up an organizing committee for the purpose of forming a Regional Planning Board for Northern Ontario (130, p. 21), and at the same conference the case for a separate University of Northern Ontario was also presented (130, p. 17). Such actions as these have led to movements to erect part of northern Ontario into a separate province, the idea of which dates back to the 1920s. The most recent of these movements comes from an organization known as "The New Province League", which advocates the creation of a separate province, tentatively named "Aurora", because it feels that not only are the characteristics of the people of northern Ontario different from those of the south but also that the development of the natural resources of the region, particularly the forest and minerals, would proceed more effectively if they were under separate provincial administration (191a). This group maintains that:

"The natural eastern boundary of the Province of North Ontario extends north from Sault Ste. Marie, following approximately the route of the Algoma Central Railway to Hearst, and thence to Port Albany. In the event that residents of Algoma and Cochrane preferred to keep their attachment with South Ontario, the boundary line could follow the eastern Boundary of the District of Thunder Bay, taking a general north and south line from Lake Superior through White River to Port Albany. In either case, such a partition would set aside a compact area unbroken by physical barriers and peopled by those with common problems and ambitions. In either case the total area of the new province would be comparable with Manitoba, Saskatchewan and Alberta. The initial population of 200,000 would be just about the same as the population in Alberta and Saskatchewan when they were first created provinces" (188, p. 5).

NORTHERN MANITOBA

Somewhat similar ideas have been voiced in northern Manitoba, where the creation of a province to be known as "Pre-Cambria" has been suggested. "Roughly, the new province should start at the Ontario-Manitoba boundary, stretch northerly along a line through the centre of Lake Winnipeg in Manitoba, shifting west at Grand Rapids on the west shore of the lake, and thence westerly along the 53rd Parallel to the Pacific Ocean". The merit of the idea was, again, that northern people would have more say in northern affairs (50a, 195a).

THE TERRITORIES

Provincial Extension. Since 1900 several proposals have been put forward advocating the unification of the Yukon Territory and the province of British Columbia. The question first arose in 1905 and again in 1914, 1920, 1924, and 1938. The supporters of the proposal had one or two main advantages in mind. The first was the reduction of the relatively high cost of the administration of the Yukon Territory, particularly because serious depopulation had occurred there since the peak of the gold rush days. The second was based on the principle that both British Columbia and the Yukon had the same kind of physical and human resources and both required similar laws for certain activities, such as mining (41, cols. 7068-9). The first argument lost much of its force when Yukon administration costs were reduced, and, in any case, the citizens of the Yukon at all times were greatly opposed to the suggestion. The probable increase in population that may come with the Yukon power developments and further mining activity might seem to promise more revenue and a better basis for a separate administration. In 1952, both British Columbia and Alberta "agreed on the desirability" of extending their northern boundaries to 65 degrees north. It was suggested that this would eliminate the difficulties experienced by the companies operating in the northwest, which had their head-quarters in British Columbia and Alberta and were, therefore, incorporated under provincial law, but which carried out their development work under federal jurisdiction (195). However, nothing has come of this suggestion.

In anticipation of the creation of one or more provinces out of parts of the Northwest Territories, which ultimately occurred in 1905, it had been suggested that the new province or provinces would "have no northern boundary other than the North Pole" (20). The Alberta and Saskatchewan Acts, how-ever, clearly indicated that this was not to be so, but during 1938 petitions were forwarded to the Federal Government from parts of northern Alberta and northern British Columbia advocating the formation of a new province out of certain parts of these two provinces and a part of the Northwest Territories— the part that had, since 1905, become more easily accessible and capable of development (45, cols. 3074-5). It was also the desire of the Alberta govern-ment to have the matter placed on the agenda of the 1945 Dominion-Provincial Conference (32, p. 33).

That these ideas are still current is clear from the remarks made by the Hon. Mr. Aseltine in the Senate of Canada, in 1953:

". . . Give the part north of British Columbia, which extends north to the Arctic Ocean, to the province of British Columbia. All the travel out of that country is through British Columbia anyway. Give that part north of the province of Alberta to the province of Alberta. That would take in the Mackenzie river valley, all that territory is adjacent to Edmonton, and all the traffic out of that territory is through the northern part of Alberta. Then, give the part north of Saskatchewan to the province of Saskatchewan, and the part north of Manitoba to the province of Manitoba" (136a, p. 162).

Lingard (32, p. 32) in discussing some of these proposals clearly does not envisage major or intricate boundary changes as being "within the realm of possibility". He does, however, consider the northward extension of the "Western Provinces" to embrace neighbouring territory to be possible, as well as the formation of a new northern province to include Yukon Territory and Mackenzie District. The possible development of provinces north of the 60th parallel would be in accordance with the policy outlined by the Prime Minister of Canada in 1912, to which reference has already been made. This statement concluded with the question "Is not that the goal to which we should aspire, that every inch of Canadian Territory should ultimately be under provincial organization?" (44, col. 4340).

Provincial Contraction. There have also been advocates of the view that part of the boundary of the Northwest Territories should be moved farther southward on the grounds that it now lies north of the area where effective provincial control and development are being carried on and that it divides an area that forms reasonably coherent territory. For example, the 60th parallel, the present boundary, passes about 1 mile south of Fort Smith, crossing the road that links that settlement to Fitzgerald. Both settlements are part of the same geographical area, which is isolated from the more densely populated parts of Alberta not only by a distance of some 300 miles but also by large intervening areas of swamp and high land. Yet Fort Smith is under the admini-stration of the Northwest Territories and Fitzgerald that of Alberta. "A truck wishing to operate on the 16-mile highway joining them requires a licence secured ultimately from both governments" (100). It has been suggested, though not on a government level, that to overcome such problems those parts of the six larger provinces east of British Columbia that lie north of the 55th parallel should revert to the administration of the Northwest Territories for a limited period of time. Such a boundary would leave most of the well-settled land in the provinces, and would not further complicate the local situation in Alberta by cutting into the area tributary to the road to Alaska. It has further been suggested that the "capital" of the area should be Churchill as "it is more important for the port to be unified administratively with the area it serves to the north" than with any distant lands to the southwest that might be also considered to form a "tributary area" to Churchill.

Whatever the merits or demerits of these suggestions, the question of transferring land within a province to territorial control is worth examining. Something similar occurred in Australia when, in 1863, the state of South Australia was provisionally extended so as to include a large area of semi-arid country to the north of it. This was partly because some good pastoral lands had been found in the area as a result of A. C. Gregory's explorations of 1855-56. South Australia had a particular interest in the area, not only because it was contiguous, but also because of the Stuart expeditions of 1860-62, which were based on Adelaide. But in spite of the valiant efforts on the part of South Australia to develop this northern area, they proved costly and disappointing, and in 1909 the Northern Territory was transferred to the Government of Australia.

In Canada, the nearest approach to this kind of arrangement occurred as a result of the terms of union between the Dominion of Canada and British Columbia, when the province agreed to convey to the Federal Government certain public lands, in trust, in order to further the completion of a railway from the Pacific to the Atlantic Oceans. This arrangement was modified and extended in 1884 by the Legislature of British Columbia, which granted to the Federal Government "three and a half million acres of land in that portion of the Peace River district of British Columbia lying east of the Rocky Mountains and adjoining the Northwest Territory of Canada, to be located by the Dominion in one rectangular block". Little was known about the area and the exact location of the block was not fixed until an exploratory survey had been made, in 1905-06, at the instance of the then Minister of the Interior (155, p. 1). From that time on, however, the Peace River Block was considered as Dominion Lands and opened for settlement (138, p. 24).

It appears likely that the reasons for the choice of an area in that part of British Columbia east of the Rocky Mountains, rather than an area in some other part of the province, were based largely on its remoteness and difficulty of access in relation to provincial administration. In 1884, even the southern part of the province had only recently acquired rail connections with the rest of Canada. No connection whatever existed with the great tract lying on the eastern side of the Rocky Mountains.

By 1927, however, the situation had changed materially. Administration of the Peace River Block had proved to be very costly, and it was considered that it would be better "if the lands were in the hands of the provincial authorities who have all the machinery available for taking care of them, in as much as the resources of the province with the exception of the lands in question are owned and administered by the province itself" (138, p. 27). In 1930, the area was returned to the Government of British Columbia.

REGIONALISM AND BOUNDARY CHANGES *separate*

Provincial boundaries may be said to have been inevitable in Canada. The geographical, historical, and political factors involved all pointed to the division of the country into regions that should be autonomous in matters of purely local concern, with a central authority to deal with matters affecting the country as a whole. How, then, were the necessary divisions to be made? As the previous chapters show, geographical considerations have always been to the forefront in fixing interprovincial boundaries. In fact, regionalism—the very basis of geographical science today—has always been an important factor in considering interprovincial boundaries, even though the resulting legislation has not always delimited the boundary on a strictly regional basis.

The definitions of a region are multitudinous but its "kernel characteristic" is that it is "an area within which certain types of socio-economic adjustments have been made by man so generally as to provide the reason for separating that area from adjacent areas which are characterized by different types of adjustments" (134, p. 137).

THE CANADA-UNITED STATES BOUNDARY

When we hear the familiar statement that Canada as a whole came into being "against geography", what is usually meant is that the Canada-United States land boundary is not a good regional boundary. From the Atlantic to the Pacific this boundary separates the physical regions of Canada from their United States counterparts by cutting across every physiographic province it encounters. The 49th Parallel cuts the west coast of Canada from that of the United States; it separates the Canadian Cordillera from the Rocky Mountains in the United States; it divides the interior plains of Canada from those of the United States, and in the east it separates the Canadian Maritimes from their counterparts in New England.

Yet it has been shown that parts of the present Canada-United States boundary were reasonable "natural divides" at the time of their establishment, for they more or less coincided with watersheds between river systems that flowed east-west rather than north-south. "The St. Lawrence waterways system and the network of rivers that fringe the Laurentian plateau (sic) link up with the river systems of the North-West in a manner that has given the northern portion of the continent a peculiar measure of east and west unity which, since the earliest days of white settlement, has stimulated a corresponding separateness and unity in the history of its development" (187a, p. 385). Later, the transcontinental railways followed them, and, in following and leading east-west migration enormously strengthened the latitudinal rather than the logitudinal forces at work. Thus, if Canadians think of the political unit "Canada" as a "region", that is, if they think of the State of Canada as embracing a distinct nation, it is essentially based on the geography of the past. But there are signs that the past may be resurrected in a new form in the future. The one physiographic region that is almost entirely included in the Canada of today is the Canadian Shield, once solely the realm of the Hudson's Bay Company. Today millions of Canadians living around its fringes derive their livelihood from its rich mineral resources and forests, which are becoming even more productive as technology advances.

The question whether or not political division between Canada and the United States is desirable, economically or otherwise, is, however, irrelevant to this discussion. Canada's sense of nationhood has always been strong, and was probably never stronger than at present. Thus it is the factor of human geography, based on historical development, that outweighs the effects of the economic and physical factors of regionalism and prevents the elimination of the International Boundary, and "inter-regionalism" between the two countries exerts its effect without political boundary adjustment.

THE INTERPROVINCIAL BOUNDARIES

But what of the provincial boundaries? First of all, let us note that the boundaries of New Brunswick, Nova Scotia, Prince Edward Island, and British Columbia, and the Ontario-Quebec boundary from the St. Lawrence to Lake Timiskaming, were established approximately in accordance with regional principles, having regard to the "state of the arts" and the economies of the areas concerned *at the time the boundaries were established.*

The Ontario-Manitoba boundary would have had a regional basis if the original views of the Dominion Government and Manitoba had prevailed; and the boundaries suggested by such men as Palliser and Premier Haultain had a fundamentally regional basis. But the various boundaries established since 1867 had little geographical validity when set up. They have acquired such, if at all, only as a result of the geographical effects they have themselves produced.

The boundaries of the Canadian provinces have, therefore, been established according to two different sets of principles. Before 1867, the trend appeared to be towards making the administrative areas correspond to one or more sets of factors of the life of the area. In the case of British Columbia and Newfoundland it was the distribution of "industry" or the general pattern of economic life. In the case of Ontario and Quebec it was the traditional structure and historical grouping of the population. In the case of the Old Maritimes it was an effort to equate the areas of administration with the zones of influence of the principal towns in each province.

After 1867, an effort was made to apply some general quantitative standard to the areas being erected into provinces, with a view to securing areas of approximately similar area or population, as well as to limit the total number of provinces to be created.

REGIONALISM AND ADMINISTRATION

The fact that the provincial and territorial boundaries of Canada have been established according to two different sets of principles raises several problems.

Fundamentally, boundaries are needed to mark off different areas of administration: and it is evident that administrative problems are different in different parts of Canada. The very size and spatial setting that made the federal structure the only workable one embrace such diversity of climate, soil, land form, and vegetation that differing types of administration are inevitable.

As a result, there has been a tendency to put forward the view that administrative areas should be based on regions where resource utilization is similar, i.e., the true "geographic region"—"an area in which the combination of environmental and demographic factors have created a homogeneity of economic and social structure" (99, p. 404).

Because of the complex factors involved, unanimity as to the specific extent of geographical regions is seldom reached, but eleven have been suggested for Canada (68, pp. 84-89). These are shown in Figure 22. In discussing regionalism and administration, one point is not always made clear, even by those who understand the nature of regionalism best, and that is that regional boundaries generally tend to be zones, rather than sharp lines. Furthermore, all regions are liable to change as technology changes, but are likely to undergo the greatest changes around their fringes. The theory that political boundaries should follow regional lines, therefore, seems unsound, for political boundaries are changed only with great difficulty, and their location in areas where changing conditions

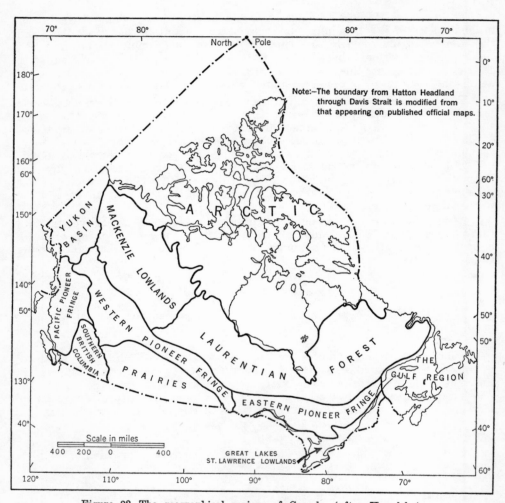

Figure 22. The geographical regions of Canada (after Hewelcke).

may lead to demands for revision seems unwise. No limits can be placed on the rate or the extent of movement of regional boundaries, although these changes usually take place slowly in areas that have been highly developed for a long period. But in the submarginal lands of Canada they may take place in a surprisingly short space of time.

Some of the arguments for boundary change in Canada have been adopted from similar arguments put forward for a more "regional approach" to boundaries in the United States, such as the following:

". . . new boundaries certainly would not coincide with the present ones. In all probability, geographic regions characterised by uniformity of resource use would be employed, for we live, produce and trade regionally. To some extent we also think regionally. Such a division would be reflected in greater homogeneity in the economic and social life of the people" (197, p. 38).

But neither in its physical nor its political geography is Canada in the same situation as the United States. It has just been pointed out that in the submarginal lands of Canada regional boundaries may change rapidly. Any political boundary based on such boundaries would, therefore, soon become unsatisfactory from a practical standpoint. Such a situation does not exist, at least not to the same extent, in the United States. Furthermore, if administrative boundaries did follow the regional lines of Figure 22, they would include vast regions containing very small and widely scattered populations. Either this small number of people would be expected to provide the taxes for the support of their administrative services, or the Federal Government would be expected to subsidize the administration and development of these areas. Generally speaking, the more sparse the population, the greater the dependence on the Federal treasury, and the greater the amount of Federal revenue from well populated areas that must be devoted to the sparsely populated areas.

If, on the other hand, the sparsely populated lands are divided among the provinces, the provincial governments will have to finance the development and administration of such lands. The average taxpayer is usually closer to the provincial government than he is to Ottawa, and such division of the sparsely populated lands is, therefore, likely to mean a closer and more sustained interest in them, even if provincial control of education and natural resources alone are considered; administrative personnel also are likely to be drawn from the province, and, of course, will be directly responsible to the provincial capital rather than to Ottawa. Every province as it exists today, except Nova Scotia, Prince Edward Island, and New Brunswick, has some sparsely populated area, and even Nova Scotia and New Brunswick have wilderness areas. One has only to think of the attitude of the people of Ontario toward their provincially-owned Northland Railway, or the pride of the people of Manitoba in the port of Churchill to realize the force of this argument.

The two sides of the question have been well exemplified recently. In advocating a province of "Pre-Cambria", to which reference has already been made, it was said "let the mining men look after mining, oilmen look after oil, and the farmers look after farming" (195a). "Merge the territories with the same kind of resources, conditions and problems into one province, and they will be better administered" (50a). Yet barely a month later Senator Aseltine said "I am informed that the cost of administering the territories is considerable and that there is very little revenue from it, so I am going to suggest . . . that the way to solve this whole problem of looking after the Northwest Territories would be to give them to the provinces that I have mentioned . . . These provinces have local legislatures and governments and the set-up is such that they could handle all this business very easily and relieve the federal government of any difficulties or expense in connection with it" (36a, p. 162). Thus, both the "regional case" and the case for diversity have been stated and "the question is whether areas which have distinct and perhaps conflicting interests, especially of an economic character, should be kept in distinct administrative units or can safely be contained in one unit" (99, p. 405).

The inclusion of different regions within provinces would lead to a considerable diversification of the economy. The question then arises, should such a diversity of interest within an internal political area be advocated. It might be useful to point out here that there may be a difference between the political geography of an independent state or country and the political geography of the divisions within that state or country. An independent state or country is usually considered fortunate if it includes within its borders a variety of regions and resources, because it usually results in greater independence and influence internationally (133). Internally, in a similar way, if a political unit includes a wide variety of regions and resources its independence and power are great. In Canada, it is only necessary to compare the large and small provinces to realize the validity of this statement. One of the most outstanding results of the application of the different sets of principles on which the present provincial boundaries are based, is the unequal influence that the individual provinces exert.

SECTIONALISM AND ADMINISTRATION

It has been said that the section is the political version of the region. Used in this sense 'section' may refer to one administrative unit at the state or provincial level, or to a group of several. The United States National Resources Committee came to the conclusion that, for the purposes of resource conservation, the best achievable administrative units were those aggregations of states that most nearly coincided with divisions based on major regions (132). It has been suggested that in Canada there is a remarkable agreement between the regional boundaries and the generally recognized provincial groupings (e.g., the Prairie Provinces; the Maritime Provinces), although this appears to be a rash generalization when it is realized that each section includes part of the same region (the Sub-Arctic or Pioneer Fringes) and almost every section includes part of the Arctic Region (Figure 23).

Because such sections have, unofficially, taken shape in Canada in response to the geography of the various parts of the country, and because they have become part of Canadian thinking and organization, it is pertinent to pursue the idea of sections *within* the provinces. The way in which the province of Saskatchewan has manifested its recognition that the problems of the northern and southern halves of the province differ materially is instructive. Since 1946, the province has had a Northern Administration District in the Department of Natural Resources, in order to bring about a more efficient administration of the province's resources in fish, fur, timber, and minerals in the far north. "A northern administrator to co-ordinate activities of all government departments operating roughly north of Montreal Lake, supervise all activities of the natural resources department, and administer local affairs in the northern area has been appointed . . . who has made his headquarters at Prince Albert" (149, p. 35). Furthermore, it has been determined as a matter of policy that all departmental personnel in the northern part of the province should be administered by the Prince Albert office, as well as the municipal problems, the work of three separate branches of the Department of Public Health, and that of the Department of Social Welfare (148, pp. 153-55).

Hence regional and sectional differences in Canada cannot be ignored for administrative purposes. Their existence may be taken into account either by changing the existing internal political boundaries by constitutional processes or by adjusting the internal administrative organization as the geographical situation demands so as to fit the existing boundaries.

Figure 23. The "sections" of Canada.

CHAPTER X

CONCLUSION

The foregoing chapters have led to four main groups of conclusions. In the first place they have shown the stages by which boundaries have developed in Canada. Secondly, they have demonstrated why the boundaries of Canada have their present geographical location. Thirdly, certain relationships between the evolution of these boundaries and geographical regionalism have become apparent. Finally, they have made it possible to enunciate certain principles upon which attitudes to existing boundaries, as well as to new boundaries that might be established in the future, may be based.

THE STAGES OF BOUNDARY EVOLUTION

It has already been indicated that boundaries are an outgrowth of historical processes. Brigham (14, p. 201) maintains that boundaries undergo a threefold evolution—a primitive or tribal stage; a mixed or transitional stage, in which the boundaries are shifting; and a third stage in which they become in great part fixed: these last two stages have been carried further by Jones (84, p. 57). These three stages, as they apply to Canada, may be amplified as follows:

(a) Stage of Loose Delimitation

(i) Tribal stage—The political progress of a group of people has always demanded that the limits of its area of authority be defined. Although such definition was naturally rather vague in the case of Canada's aboriginal inhabitants, such limits none the less existed, although their lack of definition gave them a character more resembling "transitional zones" than "boundaries" as the latter are thought of today by more advanced peoples. To such limits the name "frontier" is best applied, for a frontier is properly a region or zone, having width as well as length (10, p. 22). Any relation of such limits to later boundary evolution was entirely fortuitous.

(ii) European-originated exploration and discovery—This period usually sets certain latitudinal, and sometimes longitudinal, limits, to the next stage, the limits usually being those within which the explorers operated.

(iii) Claims of sovereignty—These were often made by the explorers; in these circumstances, this sub-stage was coincident with sub-stage (i). On other occasions, claims of sovereignty were made after the explorer returned to the government or organization sponsoring his expedition. The territory over which sovereignty was claimed was, as a rule, simply stated; it was usually defined by lines of latitude and often extended over areas that had not been explored or even, sometimes, discovered.

(b) Transitional State, or Stage of Precise Delimitation

(i) Exploitation and settlement—When exploitation or settlement occurred, the need for boundaries began to be apparent. This need was first recognized in some cases by the people in the areas concerned, in others by the colonial administrators either in Europe or in the colony itself, as the pattern of the economy of the area began to take shape. It may have resulted in a demand for more precise boundaries, or for further political recognition of boundaries, or both.

(ii) Political decisions on the allocation of territory—This sub-stage resulted in the boundaries consequent upon (i), which were then

(iii) Delimited in a state document, which marked the end of the transitional stage.

(c) Final Stage or Stage of Demarcation

(i) Demarcation—Often the state document mentioned above made provision for boundary demarcation and the means or stages by which such demarcation was to be carried out. In some cases, particularly with the interprovincial boundaries, demarcation was not mentioned in the delimitation document, the matter being left until the need arose. Often, before the techniques of boundary demarcation by means of monuments were well developed, boundary delimitation followed well-known physical features such as rivers or mountain ranges. Such use of physical features, or "natural" boundaries, obviated the need for demarcation of "artificial" boundaries. The adoption of physical features as boundaries was due not so much to a desire for "natural" boundaries as to the wish to avoid the expense of demarcating "artificial" ones. As more modern means of demarcation evolved, however, boundaries delimited by physical features became more difficult to survey and monument than boundaries delimited by lines of latitude and longitude.

(ii) Administration and maintenance—This is really part of the demarcation process, being necessary in order to preserve and keep in good order the various boundary markings.

Not all the boundaries of Canada passed through all these stages. The International Boundary and the older provincial boundaries did, but in the cases of Alberta and Saskatchewan, and to some extent Manitoba and the northern parts of Ontario and Quebec, stage (a) did not occur, and neither did parts of stage (b).

THE PATTERN OF BOUNDARY EVOLUTION

The foregoing chapters have shown that not only did the major boundaries of Canada develop in progressive stages but that they also developed in response to various stimuli. These stimuli were in accordance with a certain pattern in Eastern Canada, that is to say in Canada east of the Great Lakes, and a different pattern in Western and Northern Canada. The two patterns are linked by that of the International Boundary, which shows certain characteristics of both the eastern and western patterns.

In Canada east of the Great Lakes, boundary evolution proceeded hand in hand with settlement and development. It was a comparatively slow evolution not only because it occurred in a period when transportation and communication were much less developed than they are today, but also because of the struggles between French and British over control of the area. If political stability in the northern half of North America was retarded by the alternations of French and British supremacy, these alternations did at least allow the political boundaries to evolve until they met the requirements of the populations involved, as they were affected by the standards of living obtaining before the Industrial Revolution. Perhaps there is no better example of this than the southern part of the Quebec-Newfoundland boundary, which was moved eastwards and westwards until it finally came to rest in a mutually acceptable position. Perhaps this boundary adjustment in Eastern Canada was also due to the fact that it occurred under colonial regimes. The "motherlands" were not particularly concerned with inter-colonial boundaries. Those that resulted in the fewest administrative problems at home were acceptable to them, and as the colonists themselves had relatively little influence on the politics of the home authority, the colonial boundaries were adjusted to suit local conditions as the occasion demanded.

The American Revolution naturally affected the boundary between Canada and the United States of America, and as it can be argued that Canada as a separate political entity dates from the revolution, that event can also be described as the cause of all Canada's provincial boundaries. It certainly had a direct effect on all the interprovincial boundaries east of the Great Lakes. By causing "Loyalists" to settle in blocks in the unsettled areas of what is now southeastern Canada, the American revolution immediately created a need for sharper definition of the existing boundaries and caused the creation of some new ones. Before the revolution, the boundaries in Eastern Canada had become adjusted to the predominating economic factors in the various parts of the area. The revolution accentuated these, and also added a further factor, relating to the various patterns of life that the people of the area had inherited from their country of origin. In 1783 many of the inhabitants of Eastern Canada were either descended from French settlers in Canada or had been born in France; others were descended from settlers who had come to Canada from the British Isles or had themselves come from the British Isles. Still others had come to Canada from the United States, to which they had emigrated from Europe or in which they had been born. The revolution, then, added human factors to the other geographical factors that had played a part in boundary evolution. The southern parts of the Ontario-Quebec and the Quebec-Newfoundland boundaries, the boundaries of Nova Scotia and New Brunswick, and the separate political existence of Prince Edward Island were all due to the desire for different legal systems and different ways of life on the part of people with varied cultural backgrounds as well as varied economic organization. It is, therefore, scarcely an exaggeration to say that the colonial boundaries in Eastern Canada were regional boundaries at the time that they became established. It must be stressed, however, that for most practical purposes their evolution was complete before 1840.

The evolution of the International Boundary itself showed a remarkable resemblance to that of the eastern provincial boundaries. There were, of course, some differences in that the evolution of the International Boundary was much more intimately associated with the foreign policies of Great Britain and the United States of America, and that in fixing the eastern part, the idea of defence played a great part in the thinking of both sides. Yet, it was at the time of its establishment a very approximate regional boundary. East of Lake Ontario it separated the heartland of French Canada, as well as certain groups of Loyalists, from the United States. In establishing this division, the boundary ran for the most part through an almost unpopulated region, for the Appalachian Mountains, an obstacle to human intercourse even today, were an even greater barrier in 1783. West of Lake Ontario the boundary recognized the dividing effect of the Great Lakes, as well as the presence of professed anti-republicans along their northern shores. West of Lake Superior, the 49th Parallel, at the time of its establishment as the boundary, left to Britain the major part of the fur trade territory of the Hudson's Bay Company, setting it off from the area to the south, within which agricultural pursuits were more to the fore.

It is notable that west of the Rockies the 49th Parallel took a much longer period to become fixed as an international boundary. One reason for this was that on both sides of it the attitudes and activities of the people were much more alike than anywhere else along the boundary. For this reason, the establishment of that part of the International Boundary was perhaps less geographically sound at the time of its establishment than elsewhere.

Although the boundary between Canada and Alaska developed later, it, too, had a regional basis, dividing, as it did, the controlled land-fur economy of the Hudson's Bay Company from the Russian-controlled sea-fish-fur economy. In this connection, the exclusion of the "panhandle" from Canada showed a remarkable resemblance to the exclusion of the Labrador "fishing shore" from Canada almost a century before.

The provincial boundaries west of the Great Lakes, however, evolved on different bases. In some cases they were the result of factors of economic geography related to the natural resources of the area they enclosed. The boundaries of British Columbia were established to give the west coast colony-province control of gold mining; Manitoba was originally established to give separate administration to an agricultural group surrounded by an area in which the economy was much more primitive, although its dispute with Ontario was basically an economic one, as it was concerned with control of the lakehead ports. But the main common characteristic was that the boundaries developed either before significant settlement had occurred or very soon afterwards. Even by 1867, British Columbia had a population of only 32,000, and most of this small population lived in the extreme southwest of the province. The boundaries in this case were drawn without a thorough knowledge of the country they enclosed or through which they ran. This circumstance was not quite so marked in the case of the other western provinces, where final boundary establishment was slowed down by the establishment of provisional districts in the southern parts of the Northwest Territories. But the retarding effect of the establishment of provisional districts in the west was by no means as great as the retarding effect of the French and British conflicts in the east. Furthermore, in the west, by the time that the Northwest Territories were ready for definitive boundaries, some of the boundary decisions were quite arbitrary. This resulted from the fact that after provinces were established they would have a voice in the politics of the Canadian Confederation, a very different state of affairs from the establishment of colonial boundaries in the east, for these colonies had no voice in the British government.

Boundaries in Eastern Canada were, then, based on different principles than those that obtained in Western Canada. From a geographical point of view the former were more logical, as they were based on regionalism, which had time to stabilize itself before the political milieu became fixed. The eastern area was also better known by the time the boundaries became established, not as a result of scientific investigation, as understood today, but according to the facts brought to light by the reality of every day living in the area. Later boundary development followed the principle, if such it can be called, of dividing that part of Canada to which it was desired to bring provincial government into approximately equal areas. This was made abundantly clear in the creation of Alberta and Saskatchewan in 1905 and the boundary extensions of Manitoba, Ontario, and Quebec in 1912.

It is noteworthy also that the impulses that led to boundary delimitation were not always the same as those that led to boundary demarcation. This was, in some cases, due to the long interval of time between the two processes, during which changes in human values and scientific knowledge had occurred. In the case of every provincial boundary except those that, as pointed out above, were delimited on purely "human" grounds, demarcation was brought about by the administrative problems attendant upon the mining industry, or the need for controlling the resources *under* the ground, by establishing the location of mining claims. The remaining undemarcated interprovincial boundary, that between Newfoundland and Quebec, will also need to be demarcated for similar reasons— a far cry from the fishing problems that led to its earlier delimitation. The administration of mining is, of course, only the main manifestation of the common reason for boundary demarcation, namely, the need for the proper use of all natural resources, jurisdiction over which had passed to every province by 1932.

BOUNDARY EVOLUTION AND REGIONALISM

In spite of the differences in the basic reasons for their establishment, all provincial boundaries today are intended, on paper at least, to serve the *same* administrative functions. The question as to whether this is satisfactory or not has led us to examine the problem of how fixed boundaries are to be determined in a changing geographical environment. The older boundaries in Eastern Canada were good, geographically, at the time of their establishment, but this may not apply with the same force when considered against the total boundary pattern of Canada today, or the present state of the arts. In this sense, they might be considered as unsatisfactory as the boundaries in the west. It is often contended that the increasing complexities of modern life demand regional administration, but the great disadvantage of dividing Canada administratively according to regions is that the sparsely populated regions would be too numerous or too large in extent to be administered effectively. The problem posed can be considered in relationship to boundaries already established in Canada and then to boundaries that may be created in the existing territories in the future.

In the case of provincial boundaries already established, a change to regional boundaries would have to take cognizance of the fact that Canada includes regions that are handicapped by nature, which are in some ways a liability on the national balance sheet, and that the Federal Government has chosen to divide these, to some extent, among the existing provinces in order that the more fortunately endowed regions might share the responsibility for their administration. A result of this system has been the tendency of some of the provinces that have been given control over some part of the arctic and sub-arctic areas contiguous to them to anticipate expansion farther northward, so as to embrace ever-increasing sections of such areas. Another point to be borne in mind with this system is that if provincial boundaries intersect areas that may, as a result of technological advances, become economic regions, the provinces concerned might not afford the necessary degree of co-operation in their development.

But if the several present provinces recognize that within their boundaries they have several geographical regions, then they can attempt to devise intra-provincial administrative boundaries that take cognizance of these facts. Such boundaries need not be fixed and certainly not demarcated. In other words, adjustment to the existing boundaries would seem to be the best way out of the regionalism-administrative dilemma in Canada, and in order to evaluate the nature and degree of such adjustment it is necessary to classify the boundaries in some way.

THE CLASSIFICATION OF BOUNDARIES

Several classifications of boundaries have been proposed in modern times, but they are nearly all concerned with state boundaries. The oldest classification, and the one most widely employed until recent years, is the grouping of all boundaries into two categories—"natural boundaries" and "artificial boundaries". Natural features of the landscape, such as watersheds, rivers, and shorelines of lakes and seas, have long been adopted as "natural" or so-called "geographical" boundaries, whereas boundaries that do not follow natural features of the landscape, and that must, therefore, be marked on the ground by means of stones or monuments placed by man, have likewise been known as "artificial" or "conventional" boundaries. However, in the final analysis, all boundaries are artificial, because they are selected, defined, and marked by man, sometimes in conformity with the physical features of the area, but at other times in complete disregard of them (119, p. 74).

A much more comprehensive classification, based on four major groups or classes, has also been suggested (10, p. 25). Physical types are those boundaries that follow some feature marked by nature; geometrical types those that are straight lines, arcs of circles, and similar boundaries that disregard the physical geography and topography of the country; anthropogeographic types are related to human occupance of the land; and complex or compound boundaries are compromise lines adjusted to a multiplicity of factors. Other geographers, notably Hartshorne, have recognized the limitations of classifications of boundaries that are based upon mere physical features such as rivers and mountains, and have advocated classifications that take account of the relationships between boundaries and human society. Thus a boundary that is defined before any settlement whatever takes place in the area through which it runs may be called a pioneer boundary. If a boundary is defined before any very significant settlement has taken place it may be called an antecedent boundary. The term subsequent may be applied to boundaries that were decided upon after the development of the area to which they apply. Such boundaries often conform to major or minor divisions in the cultural landscape. At other times they were established with obvious lack of conformity to such divisions, and to such boundaries as these the term superimposed might be applied, because they have been superimposed on an area with complete disregard for the geographical patterns existing in that area. On still other occasions, boundaries are established on naturally separating physical features such as ranges of mountains. Such boundaries are the result of such outstanding features and may, therefore, be termed consequent (67, pp. 56, 57).

It is not possible to categorize each Canadian boundary as a whole because in many cases different parts of the same political boundary developed in different ways. This again emphasizes the fact that a human-geographical classification depends upon a previous study of the historical-geographical evolution of boundaries. But such a procedure has been followed (Figure 24) with the boundaries of Canada, and the application of the resulting classification can be illustrated with references to the British Columbia-Alberta boundary. The southern part of this boundary, following, as it does, a "naturally" separating physical feature—the Rocky Mountains—has been classified as consequent. The northern part was established before significant settlement occurred in the area and hence is an antecedent boundary. Clearly, therefore, the adjustments that might need to be made along the whole boundary in order to lessen any current difficulties in the border region will be much greater in the north than in the south.

THE FUTURE

There are indications that such adjustment to existing boundaries is occurring in some provinces, and in others efforts are being made by the citizens themselves to bring about this result. Such an attitude would avoid the other difficulties of changing existing political boundaries to regional boundaries. The chief of these would be the determination of the regional boundaries, which

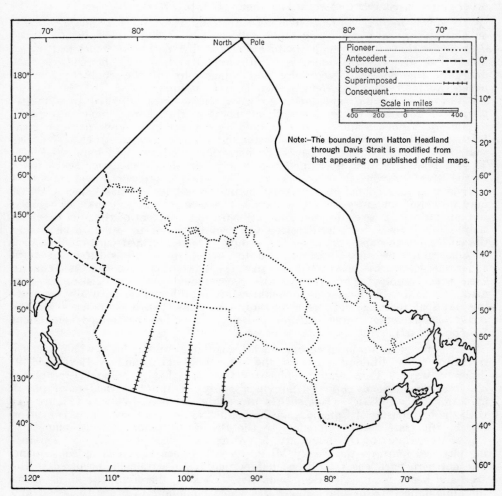

Figure 24. A classification of the major internal boundaries of Canada.

is by no means an easy task because of their inherent characteristics. They are not sharply defined, and are only valid for a given period of time, owing to the dynamic nature of human society. Secondly, a change in established boundaries would be costly, inasmuch as it would involve much new legislation, resurveying and remonumenting.

That diversity of interests is not an insurmountable obstacle at the sub-state level had been demonstrated before 1905 by the Legislature of the Northwest Territories. But if regionalism can work within the provinces, it can also function between the provinces. It has been shown, for example, that Prince Edward Island became a separate province as the result of the wishes of its inhabitants; New Brunswick and Nova Scotia became separated because of the settlement of Loyalists in the former. Newfoundland remained politically aloof from its neighbours because, in earlier times, it seemed far removed from them. But are these reasons for marked separation today? The answer is partly demonstrated by the entry of Newfoundland into Confederation in 1949. Just as its interests with Canada ultimately manifested themselves, so the regional interests of Newfoundland with its neighbouring provinces might be recognized. What were the interests of the smaller regions that took shape politically as New Brunswick, Nova Scotia, Prince Edward Island, and the island of Newfoundland have now become the common interests of a larger region best expressed by the French term, "Le pays du Golfe" (121a).

In the case of the creation of new boundaries out of the territories of today, the problems are different. The present boundaries within the territories are not fixed, and it is, therefore, here that there is the opportunity to work out boundaries that might be as geographical as possible in the light of our present knowledge—boundaries not based on ancient, vaguely worded documents or yet on purely political considerations. The fact that human adjustment to existing provincial boundaries appears to be more satisfactory than changing the boundaries themselves does not mean that new boundaries should be considered haphazardly. Sound regional principles should surely prevail in the politico-geographical evolution of the territories, if only by virtue of the fact that no matter what the advances of modern science, the resources of the territories are limited and must, therefore, be used, which means administered, wisely. In establishing any new boundaries there should perhaps, not be so much concern with equal areas as with the benefits that might accrue to all Canadians if new administrative areas were developed on a sound regional basis.

CHAPTER XI

REFERENCES

(1) Baker, J. N. L.: A History of Geographical Discovery and Exploration; London, George Harrap, 1931.

(2) Bancroft: History of British Columbia; San Francisco, 1887.

(3) Beatty, F. W.: Ontario-Manitoba Boundary; Ann. Rept. of the Ass. of Ont. Land Surv., pp. 138-139 (1949).

(4) Begg, Alexander: Statement of Facts Regarding the Alaska Boundary Question, Compiled for the Govt. of British Columbia; Victoria, King's Printer, 1902.

(5) Bemis, S. F.: Jays Treaty and the Northwest Boundary Gap; Amer. Hist. Rev., XXVII, pp. 465-484 (1922).

X (6) Bériault, Yvon: Les problèmes politiques du Nord Canadien. Le Canada et le Groenland. A qui appartient l'archipel arctique?; Ottawa, Université d'Ottawa, 1942.

(7) Bernier, J. E.: Report on the Dominion Government Expedition to the Arctic Islands and the Hudson Strait on board the C.G.S. "Arctic" 1906-1907; Ottawa, King's Printer, 1909.

(8) ———Report on the Dominion of Canada Government Expedition to the Arctic Islands and Hudson Strait on board the C.G.S. "Arctic"; Ottawa, King's Printer, 1910.

(9) Blanchard, Raoul: La Plaine de Montréal; Rev. de Géog. Alpine, XXVII, pp. 247-432 (1939).

(10) Boggs, S. W.: International Boundaries. A Study of Boundary Functions and Problems; New York, Columbia Univ. Press, 1940.

(11) ———Problems of Water-Boundary Definition: Median Lines and International Boundaries through Territorial Waters; Geog. Rev., 27, pp. 445-46 (1937).

(12) ———Boundary Functions and the Principles of Boundary-Making; Annals of the Assoc. of Amer. Geog., 22, pp. 48-9 (1932).

(13) Bourinot, Sir John G.: Builders of Nova Scotia; Toronto, Copp-Clark, 1900.

(14) Brigham, Albert Perry: Principles in the Determination of Boundaries; Geog. Rev., 7, pp. 201-19 (1919).

(15) British Columbia, Govt. of: Rept. of the Deputy Minister of Lands, Surveys, and Water Rights Branches for 1948; Victoria, B.C., King's Printer, 1949.

(16) Brown, Richard: A History of the Island of Cape Breton; London, 1869.

(17) Burpee, Lawrence J. (ed.): An Historical Atlas of Canada; London, Thomas Nelson, 1927.

(18) ———From Sea to Sea; Can. Geog. Jour., 16, pp. 3-32 (1938).

(19) ———The Search for the Western Sea; Toronto, MacMillan, 1935.

(20) Calgary Herald, December 12, 1900; March 21, 1901; January 16, 1905; February 18, 1905.

(21) ———February 7, 1905; February 13, 1905; February 21, 1905.

(22) ———February 23, 1905.

(23) Cambridge History of the British Empire, Vol. VI.

(24) Campbell, A. J.: British Columbia-Yukon Boundary Survey; Rept. of the Deputy Minister of Lands for 1948, Victoria, B.C., 1949.

(25) Canada's Sovereignty in the Arctic; R.C.M.P. Quarterly, 10, pp. 273-274 (1945).

(26) Canadian Order in Council, March 16, 1918.

(27) ———December 18, 1937.

(28) Correspondence Respecting the Alaska Boundary Together with the Award of the Alaska Boundary Tribunal; Ottawa, King's Printer, 1904.

(29) Cousineau, W.: Historique de la Seigneurie de Treadwell; unpublished M.A. thesis, University of Ottawa, 1953.

X (30) Dagenais, Pierre: Petits conflits d'une grande frontière; Revue Canadienne de Géog., II. pp. 3-8 (1948).

125

(31) Davis, John W.: The Unguarded Boundary; Geog. Rev., 12, pp. 585-601 (1922).

(32) Dawson, C. A. (ed.): The New North-West; Toronto, Univ. of Toronto Press, 1947.

(33) Dawson, Robert MacGregor: The Government of Canada; Toronto, Univ. of Toronto Press, 1947.

(34) Dawson, Samuel Edward: Line of Demarcation of Pope Alexander VI in AD 1493; X Trans. Roy. Soc., Canada (2), V, sec. II, pp. 467 (1899).

(35) Debates of the Senate of the Dominion of Canada, 1898.

(36) ———1907.

(36a)———1953.

(37) Debates, House of Commons of Canada; Ottawa, King's Printer, 1881.

(38) ———1883.

(39) ———1892.

(40) ———1898.

(41) ———1905.

(42) ———1906-7.

(43) ———1907-8.

(44) ———1911-12.

(44a)———1925.

(45) ———1938.

(45a)———1953.

(45b)———1954.

(46) Dennis, J. A.: A Short History of the Surveys Performed Under the Dominion Lands System, 1869 to 1889; Ann. Rept. of the Dept. Int. for 1891, pt. VI, pp. 1-98.

(47) Doughty, A. G., and McArthur, D. A.: Documents Relating to the Constitutional History of Canada, 1791-1818; King's Printer, Ottawa, 1914.

(48) Doughty, A. G., and Story, Norah: Documents Relating to the Constitutional History of Canada 1819-1828; Ottawa, King's Printer, 1935.

(49) Douglas, Edward M.: Boundaries, Areas, Geographical Centers and Altitudes of the United States and the Several States with a Brief Record of Important Changes in their Territory and Government; U.S. Geol. Surv. Bull. 817, Washington, 1932.

(50) Eighth Census of Canada, Vol. I; Ottawa, Dept. of Trade and Commerce, 1950.

(50a) Financial Post, November 14, 1953.

(51) Further Papers Relative to the Exploration by the Expedition under Captain Palliser; London, Eyre and Spottiswoode, 1860, p. 9.

(52) Ganong, W. F.: A Monograph on the Evolution of the Boundaries of New Brunswick; Trans. Roy. Soc., Canada (2), VII, sec. II, pp. 139-449 (1901).

(53) Gardner, G.: La Frontière Canada-Labrador; Rev. Trimestrielle Canadienne, pp. 1-18 (1938).

(54) Gilroy, Marion: The Partition of Nova Scotia, 1784; Can. Hist. Rev., 14, pp. 375-391 (1933).

(55) Great Britain, Government of: Alaska Boundary Tribunal. Protocols, Oral Arguments, With Index, Award of the Tribunal, and Opinions of Its Members, September 3 to October 20, 1903; London, The Foreign Office, 1903.

(56) ———Appendix to the Counter Case of His Majesty's Government Before the Alaska Boundary Tribunal; London, 1903, The Foreign Office.

(57) ———Boundary Between the Dominion of Canada and the Territory of Alaska. Argument Presented on the Part of the Government of His Britannic Majesty to the Tribunal Constituted Under Article 1 of the Convention Signed at Washington, January 24, 1903, Between His Britannic Majesty and the United States of America; London, The Foreign Office, 1903. X

(58) ———Boundary Between the Dominion of Canada and the Territory of Alaska. Case Presented on the Part of the Government of His Britannic Majesty to the Tribunal Constituted Under Article 1 of the Convention Signed at Washington, January 24, 1903, Between His Britannic Majesty and the United States of America; London, The Foreign Office, 1903. X

(59) ———Correspondence Relating to the Boundary Between the British Possessions in North America and the United States of America under the Treaty of 1783; London, J. Harrison and Son, 1838-42.

126

(60) ——Papers Relative to the Settlement of the Disputed Boundaries Between the Provinces of Canada and New Brunswick; London, William Clowes and Sons, 1851.

(61) ——Statement of the Evidence Submitted on Behalf of His Majesty . . . in Reference to the Boundary Between the Province of New Brunswick, in the Dominion of Canada, and the State of Maine, One of the United States of America . . . etc., Delivered December 4th, 1908; London, The Foreign Office.

(62) Great Britain, Privy Council: In the Matter of the Boundary Between the Dominion of Canada and the Colony of Newfoundland in the Labrador Peninsula; London, William Clowes and Sons Ltd., 1927, vols. I-XII.

(63) ——In the Matter of the Boundary Between the Provinces of Ontario and Manitoba, in the Dominion of Canada. Joint Appendix of Documents; Toronto, Queen's Printer, 1884.

(64) Gushue, Raymond: The Territorial Waters of Newfoundland; Can. Jour. Econ. and Pol. Sc., 15, pp. 344-352 (1949).

(65) Hare, F. K.: Regionalism: A Development in Political Geography; Public Affairs, Winter pp. 34-39 (1946).

(66) ——Regionalism and Administration: North American Experiments; Can. Jour. Econ. and Pol. Sc., 13, pp. 563-571 (1947).

(67) Hartshorne, R.: Suggestions on the Terminology of Political Boundaries; Annals of the Ass. of Amer. Geog., 26, pp. 56-7 (1936).

(68) Hewelcke, Geoffrey: Eleven Regions of Canada; Can. Geog. Jour., XLI, pp. 84-89 (1950).

(69) Hinks, Arthur R.: Notes on the Technique of Boundary Delimitation; Geog. Jour., 58, pp. 417 (1921).

(70) Holdich, T. H.: Geographical Problems in Boundary Making; Geog. Jour., 47, pp. 421-440 (1916).

(71) ——Political Frontiers and Boundary Making; London, Macmillan, 1916.

(72) Howay, F. W., Sage, W. N., and Angus, H. F.: British Columbia and the United States; Toronto, Ryerson Press, 1942.

(73) Hudson's Bay Company, A Brief History; Hudson's Bay Company, 1934.

(74) International Boundary Commission: Joint Report Upon the Survey and Demarcation of the International Boundary Between the United States and Canada along the 141st Meridian from the Arctic Ocean to Mount St. Elias; Washington, Government Printing Office, 1918.

(75) ——Joint Report Upon the Survey and Demarcation of the Boundary Between the United States and Canada from the Western Terminus of the Land Boundary Along the Forty-Ninth Parallel, on the West Side of Point Roberts, Through Georgia, Haro and Juan de Fuca Straits, to the Pacific Ocean; Washington, Government Printing Office, 1921.

(76) ——Joint Report Upon the Survey and Demarcation of the Boundary Between the United States and Canada from the Source of the St. Croix River to the St. Lawrence River; Washington, Government Printing Office, 1925.

(77) ——Joint Report Upon the Survey and Demarcation of the Boundary Between the United States and Canada from the Northwesternmost Point of Lake of the Woods to Lake Superior; Washington, Government Printing Office, 1931.

(78) ——Joint Report Upon the Survey and Demarcation of the Boundary Between the United States and Canada from the Source of the St. Croix River to the Atlantic Ocean; Washington, Government Printing Office, 1934.

(79) ——Joint Report Upon the Survey and Demarcation of the Boundary Between the United States and Canada from the Gulf of Georgia to the Northwesternmost Point of Lake of the Woods; Washington, Government Printing Office, 1937.

(80) ——Joint Report Upon the Survey and Demarcation of the Boundary Between Canada and the United States from Tongass Passage to Mount St. Elias; Ottawa, Queen's Printer, 1952.

(81) International Waterways Commission: Report of the International Waterways Commission Upon the International Boundary Between the Dominion of Canada and the United States through the St. Lawrence River and Great Lakes; Ottawa, Government Printing Bureau, 1916.

(82) Ireland, Willard E.: The Evolution of the Boundaries of British Columbia; Brit. Col. Hist. Quart., 3, pp. 263-282 (1939).

(83) Johnston, W. K.: Canada's Title to the Arctic Islands; Can. Hist. Rev., 14, pp. 22-41 **X** (1933).

(84) Jones, Stephen B.: Boundary Making, A Handbook for Statesmen, Treaty Editors and Boundary Commissioners; Washington, Carnegie Endowment for International Peace, 1945.

(85) ————The Cordilleran Section of the Canada-United States Borderland; Geog. Jour., 89, pp. 439-50 (1937).

(86) ————The Description of International Boundaries; Annals of the Ass. of Amer. Geog., 33, pp. 99-117 (1943).

(87) ————The Forty-Ninth Parallel in the Great Plains; Jour. of Geog., 31, pp. 357-67 (1932).

(88) Journals of the House of Commons of Canada, Vol. XIV, Appendix I, 1880.

(89) Keenleyside, H. L.: Canada and the United States; New York, Alfred A. Knopf, 1929.

(90) Kennedy, W. P. M.: Documents of the Canadian Constitution 1759-1915; Toronto, Oxford Univ. Press, 1918.

(91) King, Shirley: The Ontario-Quebec Boundary: Lake Temiskaming to James Bay; Ann. Rept. of the Ass. of Ont. Land Surv., pp. 143-155 (1934).

(92) King, W. F.: Report Upon the Title of Canada to the Islands North of the Mainland **X** of Canada; Ottawa, Dept. of the Int., 1905.

(93) Klotz, Otto: Boundaries of Canada; Waterloo Hist. Soc., 1914.

(94) ————The History of the Forty-Ninth Parallel Survey West of the Rocky Mountains; Geog. Rev., 3, pp. 382-87 (1917).

(95) Laxdal, Jon K.: New Iceland 1875-1950; The Icelandic Canadian, 9, pp. 17-20, 45-50 (1950).

(96) La Presse, December 23, 1949.

(97) Lindsey, Charles: An Investigation of the Unsettled Boundaries of Ontario; Toronto, Hunter, Rose and Co., 1873.

(98) Lingard, C. C.: Territorial Government in Canada. The Autonomy Question in the Old North-West Territories; Toronto, Univ. of Toronto Press, 1946.

(99) Lipman, V. D.: Local Government Areas, 1834-1945; Oxford, Blackwell, 1949.

(100) Lloyd, H. T.: The Geography and Administration of Northern Canada; unpublished D.Sc. dissertation, University of Bristol, 1949.

(101) Low, A. P.: Report on the Dominion Government Expedition to Hudson Bay and the Arctic Islands 1903-1904; Ottawa, Govt. Printing Bur., 1906.

(102) Lower, A. R. M.: What this Country Needs is Ten New Provinces; Maclean's Mag., 61, pp. 7 and 77-79 (1948).

(103) Lucas, Sir C. P.: A History of Canada 1763-1812; Oxford, Clarendon Press, 1909.

(104) ————Historical Geography of the British Colonies, Vol. V, Canada—Part I Historical; Oxford, Clarendon Press, 1911.

(105) MacKay, R. A. (ed.): Newfoundland—Economic, Diplomatic and Strategic Studies; Toronto, Oxford Univ. Press, 1946.

(106) Mackenzie, Alexander: Voyages from Montreal through the Continent of North America to the Frozen and Pacific Oceans in 1789 and 1793, Vol. II; Toronto, Morang, c. 1901.

(107) Mackintosh, W. A.: Prairie Settlement. The Geographical Setting; Toronto, Macmillan, 1934.

(108) Macleod Gazette, January 10, 1902.

(109) Macphail, Andrew: The History of Prince Edward Island; Canada and Its Provinces, Vol. XIII, Toronto, The Publishers Association, 1913.

(110) Martin, Archer: The Hudson's Bay Company's Land Tenures and the Occupation of Assiniboia by Lord Selkirk's Settlers; London, William Clowes, 1898.

(111) Mayo, Lawrence Shaw: The Forty-Fifth Parallel: or Detail of the Unguarded Boundary; Geog. Rev., 13, pp. 255-65 (1923).

(112) Medicine Hat Times, February 17, 1905.

(113) Merk, F.: British Party Politics and Oregon; Amer. Hist. Rev., XXXVII (1932).

(114) ————Oregon Pioneers and the Boundary; Amer. Hist. Rev., XXIX (1924).

(115) Mills, David: A report on the Boundaries of Ontario; Toronto, Hunter, Ross and Co., 1873.

(116) ————The Canadian View of the Alaskan Boundary Dispute; Ottawa, Gov. Printing Bur., 1899.

(117) Millward, A. E.: Southern Baffin Island; Canada, Dept. of the Int., Ottawa, 1929.

(118) Milton, Viscount: A History of the San Juan Water Boundary Question; London, Cassell, Petter and Calpin, 1869.

(119) Moodie, A. E.: Geography Behind Politics; London, Hutchison's Univ. Lib., 1947.

(120) Morton, A. S., and Martin, Chester: History of Prairie Settlement and Dominion Lands Policy; Toronto, MacMillan, 1936.

(121) Nicholson, N. L.: Some Aspects of the Political Geography of Keewatin; The Canadian Geographer, No. 3, pp. 73-84 (1953).

(121a)————Boundary Adjustments in the Gulf of St. Lawrence Region; The Newfoundland Quarterly, LIII, pp. 13-17 (1954).

(122) North Western Ontario: Its Boundaries, Resources and Communications; Toronto, Hunter, Rose and Co., 1879.

(123) Ontario, Government of: Statutes, Documents and Papers Bearing on the Discussion Respecting the Northern and Western Boundaries of the Province of Ontario, etc.; Toronto, Hunter, Rose and Co., 1878.

(124) ————North Western Ontario: Its Boundaries, Resources and Communications; Toronto, Hunter, Rose and Co., 1879.

(125) ————Correspondence, Papers and Documents of Dates from 1856 to 1882 Inclusive, Relating to the Northerly and Westerly Boundaries of the Province of Ontario; Toronto, C. Blackett Robinson, 1882.

(126) Patterson, G.: Sir William Alexander and the Scottish Attempt to Colonize Acadia; Trans. Roy., Soc., Canada (2), 10, X, sec. II, pp. 79-107 (1892).

(127) Paullin, C. O.: The Early Choice of the 49th Parallel as a Boundary Line; Can. Hist. Rev., 4, pp. 127-131 (1923).

(128) Pierce, John G.: On to the Bay; Ann. Rept. of the Ass. of Ont. Land Surv., pp. 129-137 (1949).

(129) Pritchett, J. P.: The Red River Valley 1811-1849; Toronto, Ryerson Press, 1942.

(130) Proceedings Northern Ontario Citizen's Planning Conference, 1950; Toronto, Dept. of Planning and Development, 1950.

(131) Regina Leader, Dec. 14, 1904.

(132) Regional Factors in National Planning; Wash., Nat. Res. Committee, 1935.

(133) Renner, G. T.: Political Geography and Its Point of View; World Political Geography, New York, Thomas T. Crowell, 1948.

(134) ————The Statistical Approach to Regions; Annals of the Ass. of Amer. Geog., XXV (1935).

(135) Report of the Commission Appointed to Delimit the Boundary Between the Provinces of Alberta and British Columbia, 1913-16, Parts I, II, and III; Ottawa, Office of the Surveyor General, 1917.

(136) Report of the Commissioners Appointed to Delimit the Boundary between the Provinces of Manitoba and Ontario from the Winnipeg River Northerly; Ottawa, Top. Surv. of Canada, 1925.

(137) Report of the Expedition to Hudson Bay and Cumberland Gulf; Canada, Dept. of Marine and Fisheries, Ottawa, 1898, p. 12.

(138) Report of the Royal Commission on the Reconveyance of Land to British Columbia; Ottawa, King's Printer, 1928.

(139) Report of the Second Norwegian Arctic Expedition in the "Fram" 1898-1902; Kristiania, T. O. Brogger, 1907, vol. 1.

(140) Report of the Department of the Interior, Ottawa, King's Printer, 1877.

(141) ————1880.

(142) ————1881.

(143) Rickard, T. A.: Historic Backgrounds of British Columbia; Vancouver, Wrigley, 1948.

(144) Robinson, J. Lewis: Windsor, Ontario. A Study in Urban Geography; Can. Geog. Jour., 27, pp. 106-122 (1943).

(145) Rogers, J. F.: A Historical Geography of the British Colonies, Vol. V, Canada—Part III Geographical; Oxford, Clarendon Press, 1911.

(146) Roy, Pierre-Georges: Inventaire des Concessions en Fief et Seigneurie, vol. 3.

(147) Saskatchewan-Alberta Boundary, Report of Survey to North Terminal Point, 1938; Typewritten report (not published), Ottawa, Dept. of Mines and Tech. Surv.

(148) Saskatchewan, Government of: Annual Report for 1949; Dept. of Natural Res. and Ind. Dev., Regina.

(148a)————Ann. Rept. 1952; Dept. of Natural Res., Regina.

(149) ————A Survey of Saskatchewan Government Activity, 1944-47; Regina, Sask. Bur. of Publ., 1948.

(150) Savelle, Max: The Diplomatic History of the Canadian Boundary 1749-1763; Toronto, Ryerson press, 1940.

(151) Semple, Ellen Churchill: Influence of Geographic Environment; New York, Holt, 1911.

(152) Sessional Papers of Canada: No. 97, 1905.

(153) ————No. 102, 1905.

(154) ————No. 64a, 1906-7.

(155) ————No. 178a, 1907.

(156) ————No. 94, 1912.

(157) ————No. 110a, 1912.

(158) ————No. 11c, 1886.

(159) ————No. 15, 1887.

(160) Seventeenth Annual Report of the Dept. of Marine and Fisheries; Ottawa, Maclean, Roger and Co., 1885, App. No. 30.

(161) Shortt, A., and Doughty, Arthur G.: Documents relating to the Constitutional History of Canada 1759-1791; Ottawa, King's Printer, 1918.

(162) Smedal, Gustav; Acquisition of Sovereignty Over Polar Areas; Oslo, Dybwad, 1931.

(163) Speck, F. G.: Family Territories and Social Life of Various Algonkian Bands of the Ottawa Valley; Geol. Surv., Canada, Mem. 70, 1915.

(164) Statutes of Alberta: Cap. 6, 1931.

(165) Statutes of British Columbia: 1871, Appendix.

(166) ————Cap. 8, 1931.

(167) Statutes of Canada: 14-15 Vict., Cap. 5, 1851.

(168) ————16 Vict., Cap. 152, 1853.

(169) ————33 Vict., Cap. 3, 1870.

(170) ————39 Vict., Cap. 21, 1876.

(171) ————40 Vict., Cap. 6, 1877.

(172) ————61 Vict., Cap. 3, 1898.

(173) ————61 Vict., Cap. 6, 1898 (Schedule).

(174) ————4 Edward VII, Cap. 13, 1904.

(175) ————4-5 Edward VII, Cap. 3, 1905.

(176) ————4-5 Edward VII, Cap. 42, 1905.

(177) ————2 Geo. V, Cap. 32, 1912.

(178) ————2 Geo. V, Cap. 40, 1912.

(179) ————2 Geo. V, Cap. 45, 1912.

(180) ————20-21 Geo. V, Cap. 28, 1930.

(181) ————22-23 Geo. V, Cap. 5, 1932.

(182) ————1-2 Eliz. II, Cap. 15, 1952-53.

(182a)————1-2 Eliz. II, Cap. 53, 1952-53.

(183) Statutes of Manitoba: Cap. 3, 1928.

(184) Statutes of the United Kingdom: 14-15 Vict., 1851.

(185) ————52-53 Vict., 1889.

(186) Sverdrup, Otto: New Land; London, Longmans, Green and Co., 1904, vol. II, pp. 449-450.

(187) Territorial Changes in Canada; Ottawa, Nat. Dev. Bur., Dept of the Int., undated, pp. 18.

(187a) Trotter, Reginald G.: The Canadian Back Fence in Anglo-American Relations; Queen's Quarterly, 40, pp. 383-397 (1933).

(188) The Case for a New Canadian Province. The Province of Northern Ontario; Fort William, The New Province League, 1950.

(189) The Christian Science Monitor, Jan. 22, 1951.

(190) The International Boundary Commission; External Affairs, vol. 2, No. 12, Dec. 1950.

(191) The Journals, Detailed Reports and Observations Relative to the Exploration, by Captain Palliser . . . ; London, Eyre and Spottiswoode. 1863.

(191a) Toronto Daily Star, Oct. 14, 1953.

(192) Waugh, B. W.: Completing the World's Longest Surveyed Straight Line; Can. Geog. Jour., 21, pp. 75-88 (1940).

(193) White, J.: Boundary Disputes and Treaties; Canada and Its Provinces, vol. VIII, Part III; Toronto, The Publishers Association, 1913, pp. 751-958.

(194) Whitelaw, W. M.: The Maritimes and Canada before Confederation; Toronto, Oxford Univ. Press, 1934.

(195) Winnipeg Free Press, Dec. 22, 1952.

(195a) ————October 30, 1953.

(196) Wormwith, N. B.: The Fishery Arbitrations; Canada and Its Provinces, vol. VIII, Toronto, The Publishers Association, 1913, pp. 681-750.

(197) White, C. L., and Foscue, E. J.: Regional Geography of Anglo-America; New York, Prentice-Hall, 1953, 898 pp.

APPENDIX

APPROXIMATE LENGTHS OF MAJOR CANADIAN BOUNDARIES[1]

Boundary	Length (to nearest mile)
Canada-Alaska[2]	1,456
Canada-Atlantic Ocean[3]-Gulf of St. Lawrence	10,767
Canada-Arctic Ocean-Davis Strait[4]	3,820
Canada-Pacific Ocean[5]	7,548
Canada-United States of America[6]	3,987
Alberta-British Columbia	912
Alberta-District of Mackenzie	346
Alberta-Saskatchewan	761
Alberta-United States of America	175
British Columbia-Alaska[2]	753
British Columbia-District of Mackenzie	123
British Columbia-Pacific Ocean[5]	7,548
British Columbia-United States of America[2]	560
British Columbia-Yukon Territory	507
Franklin District-Arctic Ocean-Davis Strait[4]	3,820
Franklin District-District of Mackenzie[4]	2,513
Franklin District-District of Keewatin[4]	2,017
Franklin District-Quebec[4]	1,464
Franklin District-Yukon Territory	140
Keewatin District-District of Mackenzie	508
Keewatin District-Manitoba	742
Keewatin District-Ontario	693
Keewatin District-Quebec	1,243
Mackenzie District-Saskatchewan	277
Mackenzie District-Yukon Territory	916
Manitoba-Ontario	595
Manitoba-Saskatchewan	761
Manitoba-United States of America	303
New Brunswick-Bay of Fundy	280
New Brunswick-Gulf of St. Lawrence	420
New Brunswick-Nova Scotia[7]	14
New Brunswick-Quebec	114
New Brunswick-United States of America[2]	346
Newfoundland-Atlantic Ocean-Gulf of St. Lawrence	5,480
Newfoundland-Quebec	1,714
Nova Scotia-Atlantic Ocean-Gulf of St. Lawrence[7]	2,540
Ontario-Quebec	682
Ontario-United States of America[2]	1,715
Prince Edward Island-Gulf of St. Lawrence[7]	847
Quebec-Gulf of St. Lawrence	2,050
Quebec-United States of America[2]	478
Saskatchewan-United States of America	375
Yukon Territory-Alaska	721

[1] Except where otherwise noted, these lengths were computed from measurements made on the 1951 Map of Canada published by the Surveys and Mapping Branch, Department of Mines and Technical Surveys, on a scale of 35 miles to 1 inch.

[2] International Boundary Commission Reports. For a list of these *See* References.

[3] From Cape Chidley southwards, excluding the International Boundary in Passamaquoddy Bay.

[4] Measured on the 1951 Map of Canada on a scale of 100 miles to 1 inch.

[5] Includes mainland and island coasts, but excludes water boundary with Alaska and the International Boundary through the Gulf of Georgia and Juan de Fuca Strait.

[6] International Boundary Commission Reports. Includes International Boundary through Passamaquoddy Bay and the Gulf of Georgia and Juan de Fuca Strait.

[7] Measured on a scale of 8 miles to 1 inch.

SUMMARY BY POLITICAL UNITS

Political unit	Length of boundary (to nearest mile)		
	Land boundaries	Water boundaries[8]	Total
Canada	3,147	24,431	27,578
Alberta	2,169	25	2,194
British Columbia	2,588	7,796	10,385
Manitoba	1,804	577	2,381
New Brunswick	449	700	1,149
Newfoundland	1,714	5,480	7,194
Nova Scotia	14	2,540	2,554
Ontario	1,703	1,982	3,685
Prince Edward Island	—	847	847
Quebec	2,988	4,755	7,743
Saskatchewan	2,096	77	2,173
Northwest Territories	1,879	7,885	9,764
District of Franklin	52	9,954	10,006
District of Keewatin	777	4,477	5,254
District of Mackenzie	2,513	2,170	4,683
Yukon Territory	2,144	140	2,284

[8] Excluding relatively minor bodies of water.

PLATE I

One of the mounds erected in 1874 on the plains section of the International Boundary. (Page 94.)

PLATE II

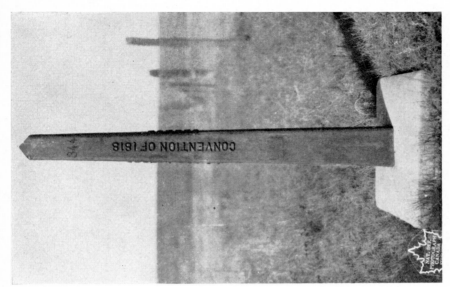

B. Hollow cast-iron monument set in concrete base used on plains section of International Boundary. (Page 100.)

A. Boundary vista and monument at Point 90 (Taku River Valley) along the British Columbia-Alaska boundary. (Page 100.)

PLATE III

B. Cedar post set in 1817, cast-iron monument originally erected in 1842-43 and reset in massive concrete base in 1908, to mark the boundary at the source of St. Croix River. (Page 99.)

A. On shore range mark ranging the first course of the International Boundary in the Gulf of Georgia, together with the monument marking the western terminus of the 49th Parallel land boundary. (Page 101.)

Plate IV

A. Scene at Parry's Rock, Winter Harbour, Dominion Day, 1909, after ceremony formally taking possession of the Arctic Archipelago for Canada. (Page 43.)

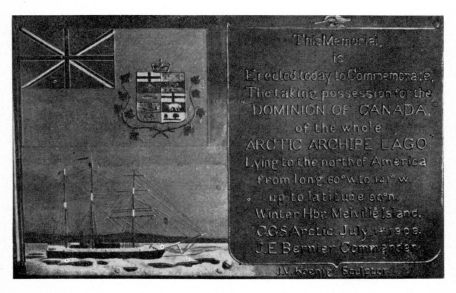

B. Close-up of tablet on rock. (Page 43.)

Plate V

A. Monument on Ontario-Manitoba boundary at main interprovincial highway.
(Page 95.)

B. Boundary monuments and road signs on New Brunswick-Quebec boundary.
(Page 95.)

139

INDEX

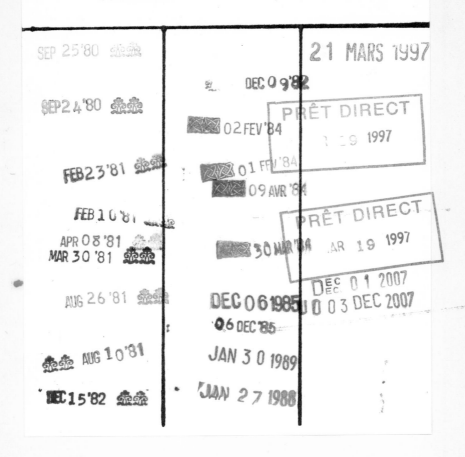